# DISNEY ENCANTO

## The Official Cookbook

# The Official Cookbook

Recipes by Patricia McCausland-Gallo
Written by Susana Illera Martínez

INSIGHT
EDITIONS

SAN RAFAEL · LOS ANGELES · LONDON

# Contents

## Chapter 1: Seasonings, Salsas, and Foundation Recipes

## Chapter 2: Amasijos, Bread, Breakfast, and Snacks

# Chapter 3: Soups and Stews

# Chapter 4: Pork, Beef, and Poultry

# Chapter 5: Seafood

# Chapter 6: Rice

# Chapter 7: Side Dishes

# Chapter 8: Sweets

# Chapter 9: Drinks and Fruits

## Dietary Considerations

| | |
|---|---|
| GF: Gluten Free | V: Vegetarian |
| GF*: Easily made Gluten Free | V*: Easily made Vegetarian |
| DF: Dairy Free | V+: Vegan |
| DF*: Easily made Dairy Free | V+*: Easily made Vegan |

# Introduction

The winter of 2021 marked an emotional moment for me and all Colombians with the release of *Encanto*. Seeing our little big country featured in a Disney movie was exciting! As a nation with various ethnicities, landscapes, music, and cuisine, we share a common bond of coming together to enjoy meals and dance as a unified community. This proud feeling transcends age and geographical barriers.

My family and I watched the film in the cold Colorado mountains, wrapped in thick throws and warmed by the memories of home. With joyful tears and far from home, we all agreed that Abuela's candle shone brightly in our hearts as a reminder of how much we cherish and long for those moments around our traditional food table, with our large families, vivid colors, music, and unity.

*Encanto* captivated us from the beginning. We relived those days of cooking together and sharing meals, united with hope, sorrow, and inner strength. The hullabaloo of Casita was precisely like our celebrations at home, where food was constantly being prepared in a kitchen full of people talking simultaneously without missing a beat.

The Madrigals' family breakfasts—which end up being more like banquets—are reminiscent of those we had at our finca's tables set with arepas, *huevos pericos, café con leche, tinto*, empanadas, *carimañolas, pandebonos*, and *chocolate caliente*. Beautiful houses built in places that resemble the magical town in *Encanto*, are surrounded by bountiful nature, birds like Camilo's toucan serenading us with their rainforest tunes, and, of course, the nonstop variety of music played by our *familia* and neighbors alike. Like Luisa in *Encanto*, it made us want to lay on a hammock the rest of the day with a refreshing *lulada* in our hand if it was a warm day or a *chocolate caliente* if the breeze from the Andes was too cold.

I treasure those memories of when cooking *buñuelos* and *pandebonos* was my role (and my pleasure!). Today, our children (and soon our grandchildren) are the ones preparing the treats, honoring the flavors and traditions of generations before them.

The enchanting town portrayed in the movie resembles our *pueblitos* and big cities, where you can find a variety of flavors, from *salpicón con helado* to *empanaditas vallunas*. With the catchy melody of tiples, guitars, accordions, and a dazzling voice in the background, *Encanto* is a vibrant world filled with Colombian snacks like *carimañolas, arepas y deditos de queso, chicharrones, butifarras*, and empanadas. It's an unpredictable dream in the middle of the tropics, with Mirabel's kind and generous soul prancing up and down Casita's stairs and Isabela's endless waterfall of flowers and colorful nature; Pepa's thunders against a rainbow in the courtyard and the delightful smell of a healing stew coming from Julieta's kitchen.

In my dearest Colombia, we are an open-arms group of diverse people, and we won't hesitate to captivate you with the flavors of our unique regions: from the Caribbean-inspired *arroz con coco titoté* and Pacific-inspired *cazuela de mariscos al coco*, both somewhat simple, to the more mountain-inspired *fríjoles, chicharrones*, and *arepas de maíz*. The love of offering food and spending time with family and guests, fully opening our hearts to giving, ties us to Colombia.

*La familia* Madrigal's tale has inspired us, mainly as it represents many Colombian families' struggles. The values of perseverance and tenacity embodied by Mirabel and Abuela Alma and fortified by the support of their family and friends grow as we learn to build a strong foundation, and to keep rebuilding it, no matter what life throws at us. The story of Encanto, woven like the embroidery of Mirabel's beautiful skirt, is entwined with her hope, sorrow, inner strength, and happiness, accompanied by hard work, music, and food.

This story reflects who we are as a community, tackling challenges together while sharing meals and embracing the power of music, which is a part of our culture's magical realism. As a close-knit society, we overcome obstacles, celebrate milestones, and forge ahead. *Encanto* beautifully captures the spirit of resilience and triumph in adversity.

The food showcased in *Encanto* is a powerful reminder of our roots and the cherished customs handed down through generations. I learned how to make empanadas, *hojaldras*, and *buñuelos* from people who inherited these recipes from their families. These individuals cherished their memories and practiced the recipes diligently. Whenever my children and grandchildren come over, they ask for "Chef Pachi's" (that's me!) Colombian dishes. And so do my sons-in-law! They indulge with their favorites: *carne desmechada*, *pollo sudado*, and *arroz con coco*.

The dishes included in this book are my homage to Colombia. Each recipe comes with step-by-step directions that are leveled from easy to hard. The building blocks we provided will help bring your flavor and twists to the recipes so that you, like the Madrigals, can add some magic and make them your own!

I have a background in food and nutrition, pastry-making, and baking. I studied at École Lenôtre in France and the American Institute of Baking in the United States. I gained valuable experience working in my mother's French bakery from the age of fourteen. Over the past twenty-plus years, I spent time abroad reconnecting with my memories of Colombian food. Through visiting people and places and learning from the kindness of many souls, I have created these recipes to share and spread love to people worldwide. I hope that these recipes will provide partners with opportunities to surprise their loved ones with Colombian memories— something that the movie *Encanto* has bestowed upon us for generations to come.

Thank you, Disney, for granting us this privilege.

## Chef Pachi
## Patricia McCausland-Gallo, CCP

# Ingredients Guide

Welcome to the Magical Gift of Colombian Cooking! On the colorful pages of this *Encanto*-inspired cookbook, you'll find a variety of delicious ingredients that contribute to Colombia's diverse and vibrant cuisine. These ingredients range from fragrant spices to tropical fruits and local staples and can be purchased online, at nearby bodegas, or at Latin mercados. We've included basic concepts and simple options to replace hard-to-find ingredients, like achiote, which is commonly used in our recipes.

**Achiote Oil:**

2 cups sunflower or olive oil

½ cup achiote (annatto) seeds

1. In a small saucepan over medium heat, place the oil and seeds and cook for 10 minutes, mixing once or twice until it begins to steam. Do not let it boil. Remove the saucepan from the heat and let it cool to room temperature.
2. Strain the oil through a fine-mesh sieve into a jar or bottle with a tight-fitting lid.

**Ají dulce:**

Ají dulce, also called small peppers (wrinkled sweet peppers) are mild, elongated green and red peppers 2 to 3 inches long with a wrinkled pointy tip. They can range in color from green to red. Commonly used in Caribbean and Latin American cuisine, with a mild, sweet flavor, ají dulce is used in a variety of dishes, including stews, soups, sauces, and marinades, and is often paired with meats, fish, or beans.

**Bananas:**

Bananas in Colombia are generally two-thirds the size of those that are exported. They come in many varieties, from the tiny three-inch bananas to those we eat daily, like the ones exported but much sweeter and softer.

**Blanco espino:**

*Ñame blanco* espino is a type of Colombian yam or tuber that is also known as *Dioscorea alata* in Latin. It is a starchy root vegetable that is often used in Latin American and Caribbean cuisine. The espino type of yam is fleshy and dissolves when cooked into a creamy white chowder.

**Cassava flours:**

There are two types of cassava flour: sweet and sour. You can buy the sweet type in many places; the sour type can be found online, but you should *not* eat it raw. If you buy them, note that they are not cassava starch, and they feel like flour instead of cornstarch.

**Chicharrón:**

Colombian chicharrón is a popular dish made with fried pork belly or pork ribs. The pork is typically seasoned, cooked in water, and then deep-fried until it is crispy on the outside and tender on the inside. It is a staple of Colombian cuisine commonly served as a side dish or a bite and can be found in many recipes as well as street food vendors, restaurants, and households.

**Coconut water:**

Coconut water is the water that lies inside the coconut, between the coconut meat. It is sometimes sold in containers that you can use to make your coconut milk, but traditionally extra water is used to complete the liquid needed to extract the coconut milk from the shredded meat.

## Colombian Adobo Seasoning and Achiote Paste Substitution:

If you want to make your own adobo seasoning, check this one out. It is a mix of spices you grind in a mortar and pestle, or coffee/spice grinder, and use it on its own or with oil instead of achiote paste. Simply mix the below in a small bowl.

2 tablespoons achiote seeds

1 tablespoon cumin seeds

1 tablespoon smoked paprika (not spicy) or smoked chili pepper (spicy)

½ tablespoon black peppercorns

1 star anise

3 cardamom seeds

6 whole cloves

2 tablespoons olive oil (optional)

**For the Colombian Adobo Seasoning:** Grind all spices and use as needed.

**For the Achiote Paste Substitution:** Add the oil to the spices to form a paste.

## Colombian drinking chocolate:

This is a very dark type of chocolate, made in molds that divide it into pieces. Each piece makes one cup of hot chocolate. Traditionally the chocolate has added sugar, is very hard to touch, and will not melt in your hands, even under the sun.

## Color:

Color is a powdered annatto seed or achiote. It can be exchanged for turmeric or for Achiote Oil.

## Concentrated bouillon base:

Traditionally, bouillon cubes were used once they appeared in markets. Nowadays, you can use the organic liquid concentrates or your own if desired.

## Cuchuco de maíz:

In Colombia, *cuchuco de maíz* is dry cracked white or yellow corn sold dried with the husk still intact. This type of corn is typically used to make arepas, tamales, soups, stews, drinks, and other traditional Colombian dishes.

## Culantro:

Culantro is also called cilantro cimarron and spiny cilantro in English and is similar in aroma to cilantro but much more robust in flavor, thus used in smaller quantities and finely diced.

## Cumin:

The best way to obtain an aromatic yet subtle flavor from cumin is to heat cumin seeds in a pan until fragrant, and then grind them in a coffee mill or mortar (used not long ago in most homes) to make your own cumin powder.

## Curuba fruit:

In English, the fruit known as *curuba* is commonly referred to as "banana passionfruit." It is an oval-shaped passionfruit with a yellow-orange rind and a tangy, tart, and juicy pulp that is reminiscent of melon. It can sometimes leave your lips feeling dry and sticky.

Discard the seeds and refrigerate the fruit for up to two months.

## Fuerte avocados:

Fuerte avocados grow in the mountainous areas of Colombia, particularly in the Andean region. They are larger and firmer, with smooth, green skin and pale green flesh that is creamy and slightly less oily than the Hass variety.

### Guanabana fruit:

Guanabana, also known as *soursop*, is a large, green, spiky fruit with large black seeds surrounded by white, pulpy flesh. It is creamy, slightly tart, and sometimes sweet. It is often used in desserts in Colombia, very often with meringues.

### Guascas herb:

A traditional Colombian herb commonly used in Colombian cuisine, *guascas* is used primarily as a seasoning herb added to soups and stews to enhance the overall flavor profile. It's an essential ingredient in *ajiaco*, contributing to the soup's characteristic taste.

This herb is known for its unique flavor and aroma, often described as having a slightly earthy, citrusy, and minty taste, which adds a distinctive and refreshing flavor to dishes. In English, *guascas* are typically called "gallant soldier" or "soldier's herb," yet they are widely recognized by its name in Spanish.

### Lulo fruit:

The fruit known as *lulo* in Colombia is commonly referred to as "naranjilla" in English. It is a small, round, fuzzy, orange, tart fruit with a green pulp similar to that of a kiwi.

### Maíz amarillo:

Colombian yellow corn, not sweet corn, has hard, starchy kernels that are not sweet. Also known as dent corn because of the small indentation on the crown of each kernel, it is sold fresh and dry. To rehydrate, soak in water for twenty-four hours, then pressure cook for one hour.

### Maíz blanco:

In Colombia, white corn (*maíz blanco*) is native to the Andean region. White corn is typically larger and softer than yellow corn and has a slightly sweeter taste. It is used to make arepas (Behind the Walls Corn Arepas, page 37; Cheesy Arepas, page 38; Hidden Egg Arepas, page 39); and bollos such as Abuela-Style Sweet Rolls (page 41) and Sweet Coconut Little Angels (page 42).

### Maíz capio:

*Maíz capio* is a type of corn that is indigenous to Colombia. It is a variety of yellow corn that has large kernels and a cob. *Maíz capio* is traditionally used in many Colombian dishes, including *buñuelos* (Healing Buñuelos, page 45), a popular holiday snack. This corn is known for its distinct flavor and texture, which makes it a favorite among Colombians. However, if *maíz capio* is not available, regular corn starch or *maicena* can be used as a substitute for making *buñuelos*.

### Mango fruit:

Mango varieties differ significantly in sweetness and flavor from unripe to ripe mangoes. Both are edible, but unripe mangoes are usually eaten with salt and lime juice, while the sweet ones are used for eating as well as for juice and desserts.

### Marranitas:

Colombian green plantain and *chicharrón*, *marranita balls*, also known as *marranitas* or *chicharrón de plátano*, are a popular snack or side dish in Colombia. They are made by cooking and mashing plantains and then adding a filling of small pieces of crispy fried pork belly (chicharrón) we call Famous Colombian Fried Pork Belly (page 85). The mixture is then shaped into small balls or patties and fried until golden brown.

## Panela:

Panela is a type of organic cane sugar sweetener made by pressing the fresh, sweet sugarcane juice from sugar cane stalks and boiling them in metal pots, which results in solid, rectangle blocks of sugar or granules. These are made in the state of Valle del Cauca, where sugar cane grows. Panela is often sold in bodegas and Latin grocery stores. It's typically available in solid forms like blocks, cones, or disks, although you may also find panela in granulated or powdered forms. But the solid one is the best quality for these recipes.

## Papaya fruit:

Papaya varieties differ in sweetness. It is a tropical fruit with green-to-orange skin and soft, orange flesh with tiny black seeds in the center.

## Pineapple fruit:

There are some varieties of pineapples where the core is not eaten, as it leaves a stinging sensation in your mouth. Many pineapples are sour, while others are very sweet.

## Seed and spice powder:

To obtain the purest flavor, the best way to use seeds and spices is to buy a bag of whole seeds and spices and grind them. In many Colombian homes, seeds and spices were ground on a circular wooden surface with a soft oval-shaped pumice rock that fit perfectly in a hand, also known as a mortar and pestle. In farmer's markets, they are sold in approximately two-tablespoon bags, so they are consumed fairly quickly and are always aromatic.

## Tamarind fruit:

Tamarind is a popular fruit in Colombia that grows on trees in large brown pods, which contain a sweet and sour pulp. *Tamarindo* is sold in its pulp with and without sugar. Try to find pulp without sugar so you can sweeten it to your desire. Tamarind is not only used for its flavor but also for its health benefits. It is a rich source of antioxidants, vitamins, and minerals, making it a nutritious addition to many Colombian dishes. Overall, tamarind is a versatile fruit that is enjoyed by many in Colombia and is an essential part of the country's culinary heritage.

## Turmeric:

In Colombia, turmeric is the root of a plant sometimes called *palo amarillo*; it is usually sold fresh, dried, or powdered. If you decide to buy fresh or dried whole pieces, try to use a stainless-steel mill to grind or powder as turmeric will stain any plastic.

## White farmer cheese:

Colombia's *queso blanco*, also known as "white cheese," is a soft and chewy cheese that is widely used in Colombian cuisine. It is typically made from cow's milk and has a mild, slightly salty flavor. White farmer cheese is used in a variety of dishes, such as arepas, empanadas, soups, finger food, and *buñuelos*. *Queso blanco* is also a famous cheese in other Latin American countries and can be found in supermarkets as *queso paisa*, white farmer cheese, or *queso blanco mexicano*, *venezolano*, and *salvadoreño*.

# Seasonings, Salsas, and Foundation Recipes

**Difficulty:** Easy
**Prep time:** 10 minutes | **Cook time:** 15 minutes
**Yield:** 1 cup
**GF, DF, V, V+**

# Familia's Sofrito
## *Guiso*

Casita, the home of the Madrigal family, is full of magic and excitement! Windows and floors dance to the rhythm of Colombian music. Be prepared for unexpected discoveries behind every door! The kitchen cabinets could be hiding enchanting recipes and miraculous ingredients that can elevate ordinary meals into irresistible culinary creations.

Sharing homemade food is a beloved tradition of the Madrigals, and Familia's Sofrito adds an extra special touch to their culinary creations. Now, you can bring this same magic to your own kitchen with our take on this traditional *guiso*, using the foundational spice of Colombian cooking to entice your entire family.

3 tablespoons olive oil

½ teaspoon achiote paste or ¼ teaspoon turmeric

2 cloves garlic, minced

1 yellow onion, diced

2 ajíes dulces (see page 10) or mini sweet peppers, seeded

2 teaspoons salt

1 cup peeled and diced tomatoes

4 whole scallions, chopped

¼ red bell pepper, minced (optional)

¼ green bell pepper, minced (optional)

1. In a large sauté pan over medium heat, place the oil and achiote paste and heat for about 30 seconds. Add the garlic, onion, ajíes dulces, and salt and lightly sauté for about 30 seconds. Mix and add the tomatoes, scallions, and bell peppers, if using. Reduce the temperature to medium-low and cook for 20 minutes.

2. Serve in small individual bowls or sauce plates with Sunrise Beef Turnovers (page 53), Did Someone Say Beans? (page 120), Magical Vision Soup (page 64), Paisa Family Platter (page 73), Golden Cassava Fries (page 123), Double Magic Plantain Discs (page 126), or inside Hidden Egg Arepas (page 39).

**NOTE:** There are as many variations of *guiso* as there are departments in Colombia. Recipes can vary in the type of onions, peppers, or herbs used. In the Caribbean coastal departments, for example, sweet green peppers and yellow onion are always present, yet on the Pacific Coast, achiote (or annatto) and green onions are the most common ingredients.

# Spice Lovers Peanut Ají
## *Ají de maní*

From the mountainous lands of southwestern Colombia, the spiced flavors of this *Ají de maní* will spread over your taste buds like the cracks in Casita! It's made by carefully grinding fresh peanuts into a thick, tasty, yet very spicy sauce.

The kids in *Encanto* might want to try it, believing they can be as strong as Luisa. But you've been warned: the gift of this *Ají de maní* is only for spice-loving Madrigals.

1 tablespoon olive oil

⅓ cup minced scallions (about 1 scallion, white and green parts)

½ cup unsalted roasted peanuts

¼ cup minced red onion (about ¼ large onion)

3 tablespoons minced cilantro

2 cloves garlic

½ teaspoon vegetable or chicken bouillon base concentrate

¼ teaspoon achiote paste or ⅛ teaspoon turmeric

¼ teaspoon salt

¼ teaspoon freshly-ground black pepper

¼ teaspoon ground cumin

1 teaspoon minced and seeded red habanero pepper

1. In a small sauté pan, heat the oil over medium-low heat, add the scallions, and cook until translucent, about 2 minutes. Remove from the heat and set aside.

2. In a blender, pulse the peanuts, red onion, 1 tablespoon of the cilantro, the garlic, vegetable base concentrate, achiote or turmeric, salt, freshly-ground black pepper, cumin, and ¾ cup water into a chunky consistency.

3. Pour the puree from the blender into the medium sauté pan with the scallions and simmer for 3 to 4 minutes over low heat, until it thickens. Transfer to a medium bowl, add the habanero and remaining 2 tablespoons cilantro. Refrigerate covered until ready to use.

4. Serve alongside Sunrise Beef Turnovers (page 53), as well as during those musical town events with Golden Pork and Beef Empanadas (page 48), and Healing Buñuelos (page 45) for a kick of spice to instantly liven the moment.

5. Extra sauce can be stored in an airtight container in the refrigerator for up to a week.

**Difficulty:** Easy

**Prep time:** 10 minutes | **Cook time:** 35 minutes

**Yield:** 2½ cups

GF, DF, V*, V+*

# Charming Sauce
## *Hogao*

This hogao is smooth and silky with a hint of tangy charm! Hogao is made with small, diced tomatoes and onions, magically transformed into the life of the party with the help of seasonings and spices!

This sauce will elevate the flavors of pretty much anything its magic touches! So get ready to spread it over an arepa, sink an empanada in it, or pour it on top of your Miracle and Love Celebration Soup (page 59).

2 tablespoons olive oil

3 cloves garlic, minced

½ teaspoon achiote paste or ¼ teaspoon turmeric (see note)

½ teaspoon ground cumin spice powder (see page 11)

½ teaspoon salt

½ teaspoon freshly-ground black pepper

4 cups peeled, seeded, finely diced Roma tomatoes (keep juice, see note) (about 12 tomatoes)

1 teaspoon vegetable or chicken bouillon base concentrate

1½ cups minced white onions (about 2 large onions)

4 tablespoons minced cilantro (leaves and stems)

1. In a medium pot over medium heat, mix the oil, garlic, achiote paste or turmeric, cumin, salt, and freshly-ground black pepper. Add the tomatoes (keep any juice from the tomato seeding process), the bouillon base concentrate, and mix and simmer for 15 minutes. The ingredients should blend into a saucy consistency. If at some point it dries out, you can add the strained tomato juice or liquid from the tomatoes or ¼ cup water and continue cooking. Add the onions and cook for another 15 minutes. Add the cilantro, mix, cook for 1 minute, and remove from the heat. Set aside.

2. Serve in small individual bowls or sauce plates with Golden Pork and Beef Empanadas (page 48), Double Magic Plantain Discs (page 126), Fiesta en el Valle Chicken Soup (page 60), and Paisa Family Platter (page 73).

**NOTES:** When seeding the tomatoes, pass through a sieve and keep the seeds and liquid.

Instead of achiote or annatto seeds, achiote paste, oil, or powder, turmeric can be used.

Cumin reaches an aromatic yet subtle flavor by using cumin seeds; heat on a pan over very low heat, until you begin to smell them and grind them in a coffee mill or mortar.

The recipe for achiote oil is in the Ingredients Guide (page 10).

This recipe is easily made vegetarian and vegan by using vegetable bouillon base.

**Difficulty:** Easy
**Prep time:** 10 minutes | **Cook time:** 20 minutes
**Yield:** 2 cups/4 servings
**GF, DF, V\*, V+\***

# Enchanting Colombia Onion Sauce
## *Encebollado*

As sweet and vibrant as a Colombian melody, this sauce made with slow-cooked onions and spices will add a touch of glowing sweetness to your meals.

The Spanish word *encebollado* makes you think of tangled onions, and it sure will twist your senses and catch your *familia's* attention with its decadent aroma from anywhere in your *casita*!

Our take on this recipe is not only delicious but also super easy to prepare. Plus, it pairs perfectly with beef, poultry, potatoes, and cassava.

3 tablespoons olive oil

½ teaspoon achiote paste or ¼ teaspoon turmeric

1 teaspoon vegetable or beef bouillon base concentrate

2 teaspoons mashed garlic

¼ teaspoon salt

¼ teaspoon freshly-ground black pepper

¼ teaspoon curry powder

2 cups yellow onions, sliced thick

1½ cups sliced, seeded tomatoes (about 5 tomatoes)

1. In a large sauté pan over medium heat, add the oil, achiote paste, bouillon base concentrate, garlic, salt, freshly-ground black pepper, and curry powder and mix.

2. Add the onions and cook covered for 8 minutes, until they appear tender and somewhat translucent.

3. Uncover, add the tomatoes, and cook for 12 minutes. The tomatoes will almost disappear into the onions in the sauce.

4. Serve over meat, fish, poultry, or on the side in a small bowl.

**NOTE:** This recipe is easily made vegetarian and vegan by using vegetable bouillon base.

# To the Rhythm of the Creole Sauce
## *Salsa criolla*

*Encanto* features Colombian rhythms and beats passed down from African ancestors. It's music that, for generations, has enticed people to jump, dance, and follow along as Casita does with its windows, drawers, and tiles.

The flavors of this salsa criolla add a touch of Colombian beat to any meal. So, get your party pants on and invite your taste buds to dance To the Rhythm of the Creole Sauce!

5 whole allspice berries

5 whole cloves

2 tablespoons olive oil

1 teaspoon achiote paste or ½ teaspoon turmeric

1 clove garlic, minced

½ teaspoon liquid beef or vegetable bouillon base concentrate

1½ teaspoons salt

¼ teaspoon freshly-ground black pepper

3 cups diced yellow onions (about 2 large yellow onions)

½ cup peeled, seeded, and diced tomatoes (about 1 tomato)

**NOTE:** This recipe is easily made vegetarian and vegan by using vegetable bouillon base.

1. Tie the allspice and cloves in cheesecloth for easier removal later.

2. In a medium saucepan over low heat, add the oil, achiote paste, tied spices, garlic, bouillon base concentrate, 1 teaspoon salt, and freshly-ground black pepper and sauté for 1 minute. Add the onions, mix, and cook covered for 15 minutes. If the onions begin to dry, add 2 tablespoons of water.

3. Add the tomatoes and the remaining ½ teaspoon salt and turn up the heat to medium-high. Remove the pan cover and cook uncovered for 10 minutes.

4. Remove the tied spices and serve over meat, fish, or poultry, or on the side in a small bowl. Add it to warm New Foundation Salty Potatoes (page 117), Magic Doorknob Meat Powder (page 74), Amazing Shredded Beef (page 76), Encanto River Crispy Fried Fish (page 98), Fried Fish Steaks from the Rainbow River (page 99), Rainforest Cassava Stew (page 125), or any other recipe to which you want to add color and rhythm.

**FUN FACT:** Salsa criolla translates to creole sauce, which, like many of our foods, originated from the mixture of European, African, and Indigenous influences. But for us, criolla refers to traditional Colombia.

**Difficulty:** Easy
**Prep time:** 25 minutes | **Cook time:** 0 minutes
**Yield:** About 4 cups
**GF, DF, V, V+**

# Dreamy Creamy Coconut Milk
## *Leche de coco*

Luisa's dream of relaxation surely couldn't be complete without a glass of this creamy and refreshing drink and a hammock.

Don't worry! You'll only need one ingredient, and it's one of the most magical gifts of the tropics: coconut—a magic ball of antioxidants that is high in fiber and low in carbohydrates. It's nature's present to celebrate life and family.

1 coconut

4 cups water/coconut water (see note)

**NOTE:** Coconut water is the liquid that lies inside the coconut, between the coconut meat. It is sometimes sold in containers that you can use to make your coconut milk, but traditionally extra water is used to complete the liquid needed to extract the coconut milk from the shredded meat.

Every coconut is unique and contains a different amount of coconut water. Shake the coconut when buying to make sure it is heavy and sounds full. When some coconut water has come out, you can shake the coconut to see if it sounds like liquid inside and pour it all out. You will have the coconut pulp left over, which can be used to add fiber to baking.

1. The coconut has 3 indentations on top, and one of them is soft. Place a skewer through the soft indentation and turn the coconut upside down onto a glass until all the liquid (coconut water) has drained into the cup.

2. Remove the coconut from the glass and break it by either hitting it with a hammer or throwing it on cement. Then release the coconut meat from the shell by placing a sharp paring knife between the meat and the shell.

3. Shred the coconut and place 1 cup of shredded coconut with ½ cup of water/coconut water into a blender and blend for 2 to 3 minutes, or until the mixture turns creamy and white. Repeat with the rest of the coconut. You might need extra water. Place the blended mixture in a sieve or a cheesecloth over an empty bowl. Press to extract the milk. Transfer to a sealed jar and refrigerate the prepared coconut milk (about 4 cups should come out from a coconut) for up to 2 days or freeze it within 2 to 3 days to prevent rancidity.

4. Serve mixed with lemonade in coconut shells or use it to make drinks, rice, soup, and sauces.

# Enchanting Scrambled Eggs
## *Huevos pericos*

Colombian families love scrambled eggs and serve them almost every day simply because they're easy, magical, and fantastical!

And when you have a large *familia* and many guests to feed at la finca (a countryside Casita), it's better to have a tasty recipe under your apron that is easy to prepare ahead of time. Farm day breakfasts are quite large family events that can extend well into the midmorning, embracing a sense of togetherness and abundance.

In case you're wondering why they're called *huevos pericos,* the word *pericos* actually means parrots. With the colorful addition of tiny tomato and onion pieces, these scrambled eggs look like the beautiful feathers of those exotic birds. It's a heavenly combination that's sure to make your taste buds sing!

1½ tablespoons olive oil

½ cup minced yellow onion, (about ½ large yellow onion)

½ cup minced tomato (about 1 tomato)

¾ teaspoon salt

⅛ teaspoon freshly-ground black pepper

6 to 8 eggs

1½ tablespoons milk (see note)

1. In a small saucepan over medium-low heat, add ½ tablespoon of the oil, the onion, tomato, ¼ teaspoon of the salt, and the freshly-ground black pepper and sauté for 1 minute. Cover, turn the heat to low, and cook for 5 minutes or until the onions are translucent. Set aside until ready to make the eggs.

2. In a large bowl, mix the eggs and add the milk and the remaining ½ teaspoon salt.

3. When ready to serve, place a medium saucepan back on the stovetop over medium-high heat. Pour the remaining 1 tablespoon oil, spread it across the pan, and add the mixed eggs and sautéed vegetables. Cook, mixing with a wooden spoon, until all the eggs are cooked, 2 to 5 minutes. Serve with coffee, arepas, or *pandebono,* and tropical fruit.

**NOTES:** Some homes have adopted the French tradition of adding cream to the eggs. This creates moister scrambled eggs by preventing them from drying out. Feel free to substitute cream in place of milk, if desired.

Feel free to improvise by adding other ingredients like green bell peppers. This dish can be made for large breakfast gatherings and offered with a variety of dairy, cured meats, and vegetables on the side as desired.

# The Magic Is Strong! Spicy Ají
## *Ají antioqueño*

Do you have what it takes to elevate the flavors of your meal to a tropical heat level?

This spicy salsa from the Colombian Antioquia region is a mysterious and vibrant red and has the unique ability to transform its shape, much like Camilo Madrigal! Be sure to watch the sauce closely as the fiery habanero pepper blends seamlessly with the vinegar and vanishes.

The Magic Is Strong! But you can keep this Spicy Ají in jars in the refrigerator, so it's always ready to add to the favorite foods of spice lovers in your familia.

1 habanero pepper, seeded

½ cup white vinegar

⅓ cup lime juice

1½ teaspoons sugar

1 teaspoon salt

½ teaspoon freshly-ground black pepper

½ cup minced cilantro
(about 1 bunch cilantro)

¼ cup minced scallions (about 1 scallion, white and green parts)

¼ cup minced white onion
(about ¼ large onion)

¼ cup peeled, seeded, and minced red tomato (about ½ tomato)

¼ cup minced red bell pepper
(about ¼ bell pepper)

2 tablespoons olive oil

1. In a blender, puree the habanero pepper, vinegar, ½ cup water, the lime juice, sugar, salt, and freshly-ground black pepper. Pass through a sieve, reserving the liquid in a jar. Add the cilantro, scallions, white onion, tomato, and bell pepper to the jar. Mix and set aside for at least 1 hour (this will allow the flavors to blend and develop a unique character and aroma). Add the oil, mix, cover, and serve. It can be refrigerated for up to 1 week in a tightly sealed jar.

2. Serve in small cups with tiny spoons alongside favorite foods, allowing people to add it like hot sauce. This pairs well with Cheesy Plantain Mochilas (page 122), "What a Joyous Day" Cassava Fritters (page 119), Did Someone Say Beans? (page 120), Colombian Power Lentils (page 116), New Foundation Salty Potatoes (page 117), Moonlight Baked Yellow Potatoes (page 118), Golden Cassava Fries (page 123), Double Magic Plantain Discs (page 126), Sweet and Savory Corn Balls (page 44), Chunky Plantain Surprise Balls (page 54), Golden Pork and Beef Empanadas (page 48), and Sunrise Beef Turnovers (page 53).

**Difficulty:** Easy
**Prep time:** 10 minutes | **Cook time:** 0 minutes
**Yield:** 2 cups
**V+, DF, GF, V**

# Cilantro Pachanguero Salsa
## *Ají valluno*

In Colombia's Valle del Cauca region, parties are referred to as pachangas. And this multilevel spicy salsa comes from this magical valley where salsa is also a musical genre that will keep you dancing all night long!

Ají valluno includes cilantro, scallions, tomatoes, lime juice, vinegar, and a variety of peppers, but since every pachanguero makes it different, you're up for a flavorful dance routine that will surprise your senses.

Our version of Cilantro Pachanguero Salsa is undoubtedly a hit that will bring your family dancing to the table!

½ teaspoon minced habanero pepper

½ cup white vinegar

¼ cup lime juice

1¼ cups chopped cilantro

¾ cup minced scallions (about 3 scallions, white and green parts)

¼ cup peeled and diced tomato (about ¾ tomato)

½ teaspoon salt

¼ teaspoon freshly-ground black pepper

2 tablespoons olive oil

1. In a blender, puree the habanero and ½ cup water, strain, and transfer the liquids to a jar. Add the vinegar, lime juice, cilantro, scallions, tomato, salt, and freshly-ground black pepper. Cover, mix, and set aside for 1 hour (this will allow the flavors to blend and develop a special character and aroma).

2. Add the oil, mix, and serve. Store any remaining salsa in an airtight container in the refrigerator for up to 3 days. Note that the cilantro may start to become a lighter green after this time.

3. Serve in tiny cups as a condiment for traditional Colombian dishes like Double Magic Plantain Discs (page 126), Golden Pork and Beef Empanadas (page 48), and Golden Cassava Fries (page 123), or use it to add zing to soups, stews, and rice.

**NOTE:** This easy-to-make salsa is adaptable to any spice preference—add more peppers for a hotter kick.

**Difficulty:** Easy
**Prep time:** 15 minutes | **Cook time:** 2 minutes
**Yield:** 1¼ cups
**V+, DF, GF, V**

# Gift Ceremony Tomato Salsa
## *Picadillo*

Antonio's hope and anticipation soar as he approaches his enchanting door on his fifth birthday.

Just as the doorknob sparkles with joy, announcing a brand-new gift to the youngest member of the Madrigal family, this charming combination of fresh tomatoes and cilantro will glow over the table, ready to reveal its magical taste to every guest at the party!

½ cup minced red onion

1 garlic clove, mashed

2 cups boiling water

1 cup seeded and diced tomato (about 2 tomatoes)

3 tablespoons minced cilantro

2 tablespoons lime juice

½ teaspoon salt

¼ teaspoon freshly-ground black pepper

¼ teaspoon minced and seeded habanero pepper (optional)

1½ tablespoons olive oil

1. Place the red onion and garlic in a sieve, pour the boiling water over them, and let cool.
2. In a small bowl, add the tomato, onion and garlic, cilantro, lime juice, salt, freshly-ground black pepper, and habanero, if using. Mix to combine and set aside for 10 minutes.
3. Drizzle with olive oil and serve in small individual sauce plates or dipping cups with Sunrise Beef Turnovers (page 53) or as a side or topping to Candlelight White Rice (page 107), Did Someone Say Beans? (page 120), Hidden Egg Arepas (page 39), Golden Pork and Beef Empanadas (page 48), Magical Vision Soup (page 64), Fiesta en el Valle Chicken Soup (page XX), or Double Magic Plantain Discs (page 126).

**NOTE:** We added the step of pouring 2 cups of boiling water over the raw onion and garlic to remove that aroma from your breath.

**Difficulty:** Easy
**Prep time:** 15 minutes
**Cook time:** 2 or 10 minutes (if using eggs)
**Yield:** 2½ cups | **GF, DF, V, V+***

# Uno, Dos, Tres Avocado Spread
## *Ají de aguacate*

Abuela's candle gave her family a miracle. It also feels like a miracle how this silky and smooth *Ají de aguacate* stays green for a long time! What helps this Uno, Dos, Tres Avocado Spread to preserve its vibrant color? The magical key is the avocado's pit sitting in the middle of the tightly sealed container, protecting the spread's texture from oxidation and maintaining its bright green color for a long time.

¼ cup white vinegar

2 tablespoons lemon juice

½ teaspoon salt

½ teaspoon freshly-ground black pepper

1½ cups finely diced avocado (about 1 avocado) (save the pit)

1 cup chopped and seeded tomatoes (about 2 tomatoes)

¼ cup finely diced red onion (about ¼ large onion)

¼ cup chopped scallions (about ½ scallion, green part included)

¼ cup seeded ají dulce, minced (about 5 sweet red peppers)

¼ cup chopped cilantro

½ teaspoon minced and seeded habanero pepper (optional)

2 hard-boiled eggs, peeled and finely chopped (optional)

**NOTES:** It will last up to two days in the refrigerator without the egg.

This recipe is vegan if the eggs are omitted.

1. In a blender, add the vinegar, lemon juice, salt, and freshly-ground black pepper and blend for about 1 minute. Add the avocado and blend to a smooth consistency, about 2 minutes.

2. Pour into a medium bowl, add the tomatoes, red onion, scallions, ají dulce, cilantro, and habanero pepper, if using. Add the hard-boiled eggs, if using, mix with a fork, and serve. Some egg can be placed on top as decoration. To keep from browning, add the avocado pit to the mixture, cover, and refrigerate until ready to use.

3. Serve in small individual or sauce plates or dipping cups with Double Magic Plantain Discs (page 126), Behind the Walls Corn Arepas (page 37), Chunky Plantain Surprise Balls (page 54), Golden Pork and Beef Empanadas (page 48), or Beef Fillet with Golden Onions (page 77).

**Difficulty:** Easy
**Prep time:** 10 minutes | **Cook time:** 0 minutes
**Yield:** ½ cup dressing / 8 servings
**GF, DF, V, V+**

# Open Door House Salad
## *Ensalada de la casa*

Nothing says *"bienvenidos a casa"* more than the simplicity of a freshly made House Salad. You can find this easy yet special salad on the side of most traditional meals at homes and in restaurants all over Colombia.

Mix iceberg lettuce—or your favorite kind—with fresh onions, tomatoes, and parsley, and you're ready! Just one more detail: the magic can't happen without the dressing.

### For the dressing:

1 tablespoon vinegar

1 clove garlic, minced

2 tablespoons minced parsley

¼ teaspoon salt

¼ teaspoon freshly-ground black pepper

½ teaspoon sugar (optional)

¼ cup olive oil

### For the salad:

6 cups lettuce (about 2 small heads of iceberg lettuce)

2 white onions, sliced

3 globe tomatoes, sliced

½ cup parsley sprigs (about 8) (optional)

1. To make the dressing: In a jar, add the vinegar, ½ tablespoon water, garlic, parsley, salt, freshly-ground black pepper, and sugar, if using, and mix. Add the oil, cover the jar with a lid, and shake.

2. To make the salad: Place a bed of the lettuce on each of 8 plates as the salad's base. Over the lettuce, arrange a couple of onion and tomato slices. Pour the dressing over the ingredients.

3. As a final touch, a sprig of parsley is often used to garnish the salad, although this is not mandatory.

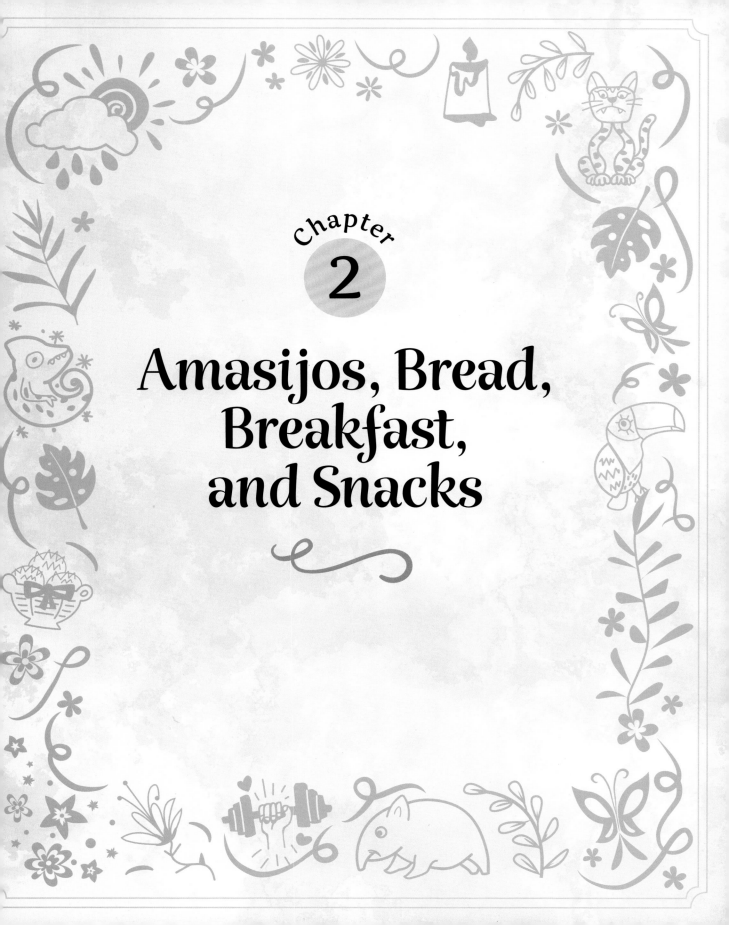

Chapter
2

# Amasijos, Bread, Breakfast, and Snacks

**Difficulty:** Easy
**Prep time:** 1 hour plus overnight resting time
**Cook time:** 1 hour | **Yield:** 16 arepas
**GF, DF\*, V, V+\***

# Behind the Walls Corn Arepas
## *Arepas de maíz*

It's no secret that, from the comfort of his hideaway and with his friendly rats by his side, Bruno indulges in the many delicious meals and snacks prepared on the other side of the walls in Casita's kitchen. Arepas are no exception!

These comforting pieces of heaven are traditionally made with home-milled corn transformed into a thin, crispy, lightly golden, and delicious Colombian arepa. But don't worry! No need to ask Luisa to bring a mill. This version is an easy recipe everyone can make and, unlike Uncle Bruno, this is one thing we like to talk about!

2½ cups (1 pound) dried white corn kernels (maíz pilado)

¼ cup sunflower oil or spray oil, for the baking pan

16 ounces white farmer cheese, for serving (optional)

4 tablespoons softened butter, for serving (optional)

Salt, for serving (optional)

**NOTES:** Flattening the dough with a tortilla press will result in a thinner arepa.

To freeze, place parchment paper between each arepa and then pack them in a tightly sealed container.

This recipe is easily made dairy free and vegan by omitting the cheese and butter.

**Day 1**

1. Rinse the dry corn kernels with water. Transfer to a bowl, cover with water, and let them sit for 24 hours.

**Day 2**

2. Drain the corn and discard the water. Place in a pressure cooker with 10 cups of water and cook for 1 hour. Release the pressure, uncover, and drain water from the corn. You will have about 8 cups of corn.

3. Process the corn in small batches (½ to 1 cup at a time) with a food processor, transfer to a bowl, and cover with a kitchen towel. When all the corn has been processed, transfer it to your counter and form a ball.

4. Transfer the ball to parchment paper and roll it into a 3-inch-wide log, cut it into 16 same-size pieces, cover, and, removing a bit at a time, form round balls of about 2 inches, keeping both the rolled balls and the cut pieces covered. Press each piece between 2 sheets of parchment paper and use a heavy pan or pot cover to flatten to ¼ inch thickness. Stack the uncooked arepas, divided with parchment. (You could freeze them now for later use.)

5. **Oven method:** Preheat the oven to 350°F. Place the arepas on a lightly oiled (about 2 tablespoons sunflower oil) or sprayed baking pan and bake for 8 minutes per side.

6. **Stovetop method:** Place the arepas one by one on a lightly oiled medium pan over medium-low heat and cook for about 5 minutes, until they look dry and lightly golden on the outside. Turn and repeat with the other side.

7. **To serve:** Serve with cheese, butter, and salt on the side to add, sprinkle, and spread to each one as desired by each person eating them. These make delicious afternoon snacks or a great breakfast with eggs.

# Cheesy Arepas
## *Arepas con queso*

Gifted with the power of healing, Julieta can make you feel better with just one arepa (or anything she cooks). Soft and delicious, with cheese oozing out from the middle, arepas taste like the miracle that will heal your soul.

*La familia* Madrigal (and almost everyone in Colombia) frequently serves these golden corn cakes at any celebration meal. Arepas are usually prepared daily for breakfast, but you can find them on street carts ready to enjoy with a variety of toppings.

This recipe for *Arepas con queso*, which can differ depending on the town in Colombia, will make you feel ready for any day ahead.

1 cup precooked white cornmeal

1 cup hot water (almost boiling)

4 tablespoons soft butter

½ teaspoon salt

¼ pound (about ⅔ cup) grated white farmer cheese (see note)

1 tablespoon olive oil or 2 tablespoons butter, for cooking

6 slices of soft farmer cheese or mozzarella

**NOTES:** This recipe is dairy-free and vegan if served without the cheese and butter.

Farmer cheese can vary in the amount of salt it contains. If you have a very salty cheese, keep the amount of salt in the recipe as is. Otherwise, you can add extra salt to taste when serving.

1. Place the cornmeal, water, butter, and salt in a large bowl and mix with a fork for 30 seconds until all ingredients are hydrated and form a paste. Cover and set aside for 5 minutes. Turn onto a work surface and knead the masa with your hands for about 2 minutes to make a smooth ball of dough. Add the grated cheese and knead for 2 minutes more.

2. Divide the dough into 6 small balls. Place each piece between 2 sheets of parchment paper or plastic and softly flatten with your hands (or flatten with a flat pot) to ½ inch thick.

3. Oil a grill or large pan with the olive oil or butter and cook the arepas over medium heat for about 3 minutes per side, or bake at 350°F until golden brown on both sides, about 10 minutes. Cut in half horizontally, add a slice of the soft cheese, and serve immediately on its own or as part of a complete breakfast with eggs, juice, or coffee.

# Hidden Egg Arepas
## *Arepas con huevo*

The Madrigal's Casita is filled with charming and wondrous details waiting to be discovered. There's magic hiding in every corner! And this same magic is also experienced on your taste buds when you take a bite of an *Arepa con huevo.*

Hiding inside a pocket made of sweet and decadent corn is an egg cooked to perfection and ready to impress your family and guests.

Treat your *familia* to a hearty breakfast dish that originated in the Caribbean towns of Colombia. This culinary wonder is a traditional favorite that will leave you feeling satisfied and ready for an enchanting day.

1½ cups precooked white cornmeal

2 teaspoons salt

1½ cups hot tap water (about 140°F)

5 cups sunflower oil, for frying

6 whole eggs

Cooked ground beef (optional)

Charming Sauce (page 19) (optional)

### Specialty Tools
Kitchen or candy thermometer

> **NOTE:** Tinto coffee cups are tiny coffee cups the size of espresso cups but used for drinking black coffee, not espresso.

1. In a large bowl, mix the cornmeal and salt. Add the hot water and mix with a fork for about 1 minute or until you have a thick and soft ball of dough. Cover it with a kitchen towel, and let it rest for 10 to 15 minutes.

2. Turn the ball of dough onto a work surface and knead for 3 minutes. Roll the dough into a 2-inch-thick log, and divide into 6 equal pieces about ¼ cup each, and a smaller 2 tablespoon piece for later use. Roll into balls, and cover with a kitchen towel. Place each piece between 2 sheets of parchment paper or plastic wrap and softly flatten to ⅓-inch thickness. Repeat this process for each ball of dough. Cover with a kitchen towel and set aside.

3. Line a plate with paper towels. Heat a heavy and deep pot with the oil (ensure it is more than 4 inches of oil) to 325°F. Carefully slide the arepas into the pot one at a time. Cook each arepa for approximately 1½ minutes on each side until they turn lightly golden, taking care not to let them crack or break apart. As they cook, they should puff up on one side in the oil, which is a sign that they are ready to be removed. Remove the arepas with a slotted spoon, inflated side up, drain, and place on the prepared plate to soak up any excess oil.

4. Using scissors or a knife, carefully make a 1-inch incision on one edge of an arepa, going all the way in until you reach the pocket of air formed on one side. Crack a whole egg into a small tinto coffee cup (see note) and pour it into the arepa's pocket. Add 1 to 2 tablespoonfuls of the cooked ground beef or Charming Sauce (page 19), if desired. Seal the opening with a piece of uncooked dough, ensuring that it's firmly closed. Carefully place the arepas back in the hot oil, and fry for an additional 2 minutes on each side until they are golden brown and crispy. Drain on a paper towel–lined plate and serve. Repeat with the remaining balls of dough. For the best flavor and texture, serve the arepas immediately while they're still hot.

# Sweet Corncakes
## *Arepas de choclo*

With every step Isabela takes, she grows beautiful plants and flowers. Their floral perfume combines with the sweet aroma from her mom Julieta's kitchen, where she prepares Arepas de choclo for the entire family.

Warm and cheesy, each bite of these traditional sweet corncakes with savory farmer cheese carries a unique taste and aroma that echoes the region's flavors where much of the corn and coffee are grown and takes your senses on a trip to the magical place called Encanto.

12 ounces (2¼ cups) white farmer cheese

2¼ cups fresh sweet corn kernels (from about 2 large ears of corn)

3 tablespoons caramel from Wobbly Andean Coffee Crème (page 142)

¼ teaspoon salt

Oil spray or butter, for cooking

**NOTES:** The arepa will be very delicate. To flip it, you can cover it with a parchment-lined plate, flip, and slide it back into the pan to finish cooking.

Decrease the heat if the arepas are too dark when you flip them.

If using frozen corn, place over a sieve, drain, and set aside until it reaches room temperature. Remove any excess moisture with paper towels. To dry out, it's best if you leave the corn in the sieve and refrigerate it overnight.

1. In a food processor, finely grind half of the cheese, place in a large bowl, and set aside.

2. Using the same processor, grind the corn for 1 to 2 minutes until all the kernels are ground. Transfer the ground corn to the bowl with the cheese, add the caramel, and salt and mix with a fork to a pancake consistency.

3. Spray or butter a medium nonstick pan and spatula, place the pan over medium-low heat, and pour ½ cup of the corn mixture, as you would with pancakes. Flatten with the prepared spatula because the mixture won't quickly spread on its own. Cover and cook until lightly golden on the bottom, about 4 minutes. Uncover and turn over to finish cooking for another 2 minutes.

4. Slice the rest of the cheese into ¼ inch thickness and about 5 by 2 inches in size. Slide the arepas onto a plate and add 1 slice of cheese, fold in half like an omelet, and serve with Heartwarming Cocoa Hug (page 159).

**Difficulty:** Medium
**Prep time:** 15 minutes (with fresh corn kernels)
**Cook time:** 1 hour
**Yield:** 3 to 4 rolls | **GF, DF, V, V+**

✸ BOLLOS AND ROLLS

# Abuela-Style Sweet Rolls
## *Bollos de mazorca*

Colombian *abuelas* have a special gift for creating heartwarming and unforgettable dishes for their loved ones, and their secret recipes are treasured through the generations.

Alma Madrigal might have loved preparing sweet corn rolls like these for her husband Pedro, their children, and grandchildren in *Encanto*.

*Bollos de mazorca* are made by tightly packing corn dough into corn husks and tying them with twine, giving them the appearance of corncobs freshly plucked from their stalks. These rolls originated in northern Colombia and Caribbean towns and are a popular treat found in many eateries and markets. We are delighted to share our adaptation of this beloved dish with you.

6 cups fresh green corn kernels
(about 6 large ears of corn)

1 teaspoon sugar

½ teaspoon salt

1 pack fresh or dry corn husks for
cooking (see note)

Butter and white farmer cheese, for
serving (optional)

**NOTES:** If fresh or dry corn husks are unavailable, you can use cooking plastic wrap as a substitute. Cut 8-by-10-inch rectangles, add the corn mix, roll, and tie the ends. Seal the sides and ends to prevent leaking.

To reheat, either steam the sliced pieces, or microwave 15 seconds after sprinkling with water.

1. In a food processor, grind the fresh corn to a grainy thick mix, about 2 cups; transfer to a large bowl, add the sugar and the salt, and mix. This mixture will be somewhat wet.

2. Arrange 1 corn husk in the palm of your hand, fold 1 inch of the husk upward to create an L shape to keep the roll masa from leaking out during the cooking process. Place ¾ cup of the corn mixture on the corn husk with the end folded. Cover with one or two other corn husks, then fold the top like an envelope. Tie with twine and set aside flat. Traditional *bollos* made in husks are about 1½ inches in diameter.

3. Fill a large pot with water and bring to a boil over high heat. Place the rolls standing up in the pot, ensuring they are fully covered with water, and simmer, covered, for 45 minutes to 1 hour. They should feel set or hard to the touch.

4. Remove from the pot and set aside for 5 minutes, cut the twine open, and slice to serve with butter and white farmer cheese on the side. Keep refrigerated and whole until ready to serve. Slice when needed.

**Difficulty:** Hard
**Prep time:** 1 hour plus overnight resting time
**Cook time:** 1 hour | **Yield:** 8 rolls
(portions of approximately ¾ cup each)
**GF, DF\*, V, V+\***

# Sweet Coconut Little Angels
## *Bollos de angelito*

These coconut-and-cheese-filled bites with a hint of anise seed are known as Bollos de angelito. They are a favorite among children, perhaps even the Madrigal primos. Initially made during Colombia's Día de Angelitos, abuelas in the Caribbean region would prepare these Sweet Coconut Little Angels to celebrate with the community.

Bollos de angelito are now available year-round and are the perfect snack for days when the children, like Mirabel, would play the accordion, sing, and dance along with the tiles in Casita.

2½ cups (1 pound) dried white corn kernels (maíz pilado) (see note)

1 cup (5 ounces) white farmer cheese

2 cups grated fresh coconut meat

¼ cup sugar

1 tablespoon anise seeds

2 teaspoons of salt

One pack dry corn husks (see note)

**NOTES:** This recipe is dairy-free and vegan if prepared without the cheese.

Dried corn kernels are often available in Latin markets.

If corn husks are unavailable, you can use "corn stick bread" silicone pans. Fill them with the corn mix, cover with foil, then place them on a pan with ½-inch water and steam them in the oven at 300°F for about 45 minutes, or until firm.

Day 1

1. On the day before making the bollos, wash the dried corn kernels, transfer to a bowl, cover with water, and let them sit for 24 hours.

Day 2

2. In a pressure cooker with 8 cups of water, cook the corn for 1 hour, drain the water, and set the corn aside to cool. If a pressure cooker is not available, you can cook the corn in a large pot by covering it with water and simmering for 4 to 5 hours.

3. In a food processor, process half of the cheese, place in a large bowl, and set aside. Cut the other half into pieces about 3 inches long and ¼ inch in diameter. Process the corn in 1-to-1½-cup batches into a smooth paste. Transfer to the bowl with the processed cheese, add the coconut, sugar, anise, and salt, and mix well with your hands. This mixture will be sticky but firm. Turn onto a worktable, cut into 8 parts, and with your hands roll to make 1-inch-wide by 3-inch-long rolls.

4. Arrange 1 corn husk in the palm of your hand, fold 1 inch of the husk upward to create an L shape to keep the masa from leaking out during the cooking process. Place one roll on the corn husk with the end folded. Cover with one or two other corn husks, then fold the top like an envelope. Tie with twine and set aside flat. Traditional bollos made in husks are about 1 inch in diameter and 3 to 4 inches long.

5. Fill a large pot with water and bring to a boil over high heat. Place the rolls standing up in the bottom of the pot, ensuring that they are fully covered in water, and simmer, covered, for 30 to 45 minutes. They should feel set or hard to the touch. Remove from the water and let rest for 5 minutes; cut the twine, open, and set aside for 10 minutes.

6. Serve in slices, warm or cold, alone or with white farmer cheese or Colombian sour cream, called suero.

# Sweet and Savory Corn Balls
## *Buñuelos de maíz*

**Difficulty:** Easy
**Prep time:** 15 minutes | **Cook time:** 5 minutes
**Yield:** 12 balls
**GF, DF, V**

Surrounded by music and candlelight, Alma and Pedro's love ignites as they take a bite of *buñuelos* in *Encanto*.

*Buñuelos* are known and loved by many because these delicious and easy-to-make corn fritters perfectly represent Colombia's lively culture. They're also called *masitas* in some places and have a sweet and savory taste from combining sweet corn with dry, salty cheese.

*Buñuelos* can be made in various shapes and sizes by dropping spoonfuls of batter or using a pastry bag to pipe them into hot oil. As they cook, the fritters appear to dance while they rise to the surface, like Casita's tiles dance when the music is on!

2 cups fresh corn kernels (about 2 large ears) (see note)

1 egg

2 tablespoons sugar

1 teaspoon salt

2 to 3 cups sunflower oil, for frying

⅓ cup yellow corn masa, if using frozen corn

### Specialty Tools:
Kitchen thermometer

1. In a blender, blend the corn kernels, egg, sugar, and salt until a homogeneous but slightly rough consistency is achieved. Transfer the mixture to a medium bowl.

2. Line a plate with paper towels. In a deep, heavy pot over medium heat, bring the oil to 350°F. Using a tablespoon, drop spoonfuls of the mixture into the oil, making sure they don't touch each other. (They should float upward. If they don't, increase the heat.) Fry until lightly golden, about 20 seconds for small 1-inch balls and up to 1 minute for larger ones, then turn and fry on the other side. Remove the fritters from the oil and drain on the prepared plate. Serve warm. These sweet yellow buñuelos are served as a side or as an appetizer on wood serving platters at gatherings.

**NOTES:** Make sure the oil has reached 350°F before adding the *buñuelos,* and don't overcrowd the pot. The way to test the oil's temperature is to drop a tiny bit of batter into it. If it's hot enough, the batter will float back up as soon as it touches the bottom of the pan.

The fritters should feel light when cooked through.

If using frozen corn kernels, set them aside until they reach room temperature, drain and dry the corn kernels, then set aside over a sieve until ready to use. Then you will add ⅓ cup of yellow corn masa and 1 tablespoon of extra sugar to the recipe.

When cutting off the corn kernels, slide your knife softly down the ear, to avoid cutting the white part of the cob, which is bitter.

**Difficulty:** Medium
**Prep time:** 15 minutes | **Cook time:** 15 minutes
**Yield:** 12 buñuelos
**GF, V**

# Healing Buñuelos
## *Buñuelos*

Julieta's recipes are remedies for real! These Healing Buñuelos, inspired by traditional Colombian holiday foods, are light and airy fritters that will remedy your hunger . . . and the Encanto townspeople's black eyes and broken wrists!

Buñuelos are meant to be shared among friends and family, especially during the holidays. Here is the magical gift of an easy-to-make recipe for buñuelos that can be prepared in advance and served at room temperature when your familia arrives to visit.

2 cups (10 ounces) very finely grated white farmer cheese

⅓ cup cornstarch (or capio starch, large white corn cornstarch)

2 tablespoons cassava starch

1 large egg

2 teaspoons sugar

½ teaspoon salt

4 to 6 cups sunflower oil, for frying

### Specialty Tools:
Kitchen thermometer

1. Place the finely grated cheese in a large bowl. Add the cornstarch, cassava starch, egg, sugar, and salt. Mix softly with your hands so it forms a light dough. Form into about ¾-inch balls. They will expand. To form the buñuelo, softly roll them between the palms of your hands. The mixture should feel light, almost like cotton balls.

2. Line a plate with paper towels. In a deep pot over medium heat, bring the oil to 350°F. Place about 6 to 8 buñuelos at a time in the oil. They should float after about 30 seconds. Decrease the heat to low, about 300°F, cook for 3 to 5 minutes, cover the pot for 5 minutes more, remove the cover, and increase the temperature to 325°F. Keep cooking, uncovered, for 5 minutes, turning if they don't turn themselves. (They should turn by themselves.) Remove from the oil and set on the prepared plate to drain. Serve.

**NOTES:** To test the temperature of the oil in a traditional way, we do the following: form a ½-inch ball of masa and place it in the oil. It should fall to the bottom of the oil and float right back up after 20 seconds. If it floats immediately, decrease the temperature of the oil.

When you fry your *buñuelos,* they should fit loosely in the pot because they expand as they cook. This way, they will turn themselves and cook evenly on all sides.

If they shrink after frying, that means they need more cooking time at a lower temperature. They might crack and create little balls on the side, but that is fine; the little balls sticking out of *Healing Buñuelos* are crispy and fun too.

**Difficulty:** Easy
**Prep time:** 40 minutes
**Cook time:** 5 to 7 minutes
**Yield:** 60 pastries | **V**

# Magical Realism Pastries
## *Hojaldras*

Colombian cuisine embodies the concept of magical realism by making everyday food fantastical and charming. Hojaldras are crispy, sweet, and savory pastries that are thinly rolled and then fried to become a bubbly canvas to decorate with a sprinkle of magic or, in nonfictional terms, powdered sugar.

They are traditionally served as dessert at holiday and family gatherings, such as the Madrigals' gift ceremonies or a dinner party with the Guzmáns. No matter the occasion, Hojaldras are always a sweet way to celebrate.

2 cups flour, plus extra for rolling

½ teaspoon salt

1 tablespoon sugar

3 tablespoons butter, very cold

6 tablespoons orange juice

2 to 3 cups sunflower oil, for frying

½ cup powdered sugar, for sprinkling

### Specialty Tools:

Kitchen thermometer

**NOTE:** This is the perfect sweet touch for the Miracle and Love Celebration Soup (page 59).

1. In a food processor pulse the flour, salt, and sugar until combined. Add the butter and orange juice and process until it forms a dough and separates from the side of the processor bowl. Set the dough aside on the counter, covered with a kitchen towel for 30 minutes.

2. Roll the dough out on a working space sprinkled with some flour to about ¼-inch thickness. Cut the dough into 60 two-by-one-inch diamond shapes and roll each piece individually to ⅛-inch thickness until you can almost see through it.

3. Line a plate with paper towels. In a heavy pot over medium-high heat, pour in the oil, bring it to 350°F, and fry the pastries until lightly golden, about 30 seconds per side. Remove them from the oil and place on the prepared plate to drain. Tap to make sure they are crispy.

4. Sprinkle the pastries with powdered sugar and serve them immediately or allow them to cool and store in airtight containers.

**Difficulty:** Medium Hard
**Prep time:** 45 minutes | **Cook time:** 15 minutes
**Yield:** 24 to 36 empanadas
**GF, DF**

# Golden Pork and Beef Empanadas
## *Empanadas vallunas*

Listen up! It's time for a grandkid roundup! And with a large platter of freshly made *Empanadas vallunas* at the table, you wouldn't need to call Dolores, Isabela, Luisa, Camilo, Mirabel, and Antonio twice!

Crispy, golden, and filled with pork, beef, and potato, our empanadas recipe skips precooking the masa for easier and faster preparation. Originally from Colombia's Valle del Cauca, these empanadas are small, two-inch fritters that make perfect finger food for the Madrigal family and yours to enjoy.

### For the meat filling

2 tablespoons olive oil

2 cloves garlic, mashed

1 teaspoon achiote paste or ½ teaspoon turmeric

½ teaspoon cumin

½ teaspoon freshly-ground black pepper

½ pound pork butt, fat removed, cut in ¼ inch dice (see note)

1 pound beef skirt steak, cut in ¼ inch dice

1 small yellow onion, diced

1½ teaspoons beef bouillon base concentrate

1 teaspoon salt

1 recipe Charming Sauce (page 19)

2 cups peeled and diced yellow or fingerling potatoes, ½-inch dice (about twelve 1 inch potatoes) (see note)

1½ cups peeled and diced red potatoes, ½-inch dice

1½ cups peeled and diced russet potatoes, ½-inch dice

### For the masa or dough

4 cups precooked yellow cornmeal

2 teaspoons achiote paste or 1 teaspoon turmeric

1 tablespoon salt

½ teaspoon cumin

6 cups hot tap water

6 tablespoons plus 2 quarts sunflower oil

Lime wedges and ají, for serving

### Specialty Tools:

Kitchen thermometer

**NOTES:** Golden Pork and Beef Empanadas can also be made with beef only.

Fry each batch with a small 1-inch piece of carrot in the oil. Through word of mouth, elders say it keeps the empanadas from coming out greasy.

If you want to cool the filling quickly, transfer it onto a baking sheet and spread it out.

You might need to buy ¾ to 1 pound of pork meat to obtain ½ pound of lean pork with visible fat removed.

Yellow potatoes, also known as Peruvian potatoes, impart a unique flavor and a creamy consistency to the filling, preventing it from oozing out of the empanada. If using fingerling potatoes, cook them until they are almost mushy, then mash them and reintroduce them into the mixture.

Why use a coffee cup or a cookie cutter? Because coffee cups have wider edges for a better seal.

To store, freeze the empanadas in single layers and bake them frozen on oiled racks over baking pans.

1. To make the meat filling: In the bowl of a pressure cooker, place the oil, garlic, achiote paste, cumin, and freshly-ground black pepper, and mix. Add the pork and beef, mix, and set aside for about 10 minutes. Add 1¾ cups water, the onion, bouillon base, and salt to the cooker, and pressure cook for 30 minutes.

2. Prepare the Charming Sauce, if you haven't already, and set aside.

3. Remove the meats from the pot and set aside in a 4-quart bowl. Add the potatoes to the liquid remaining in the pressure cooker pot. Cook on the sauté function over medium-low heat, uncovered, for 15 minutes or until they become almost mushy. With a sieve, carefully drain any leftover liquid from the pot. Add the meat mixture and Charming Sauce into the pot and mix everything together. Set aside to cool.

4. To make the masa or dough: In the bowl of a stand mixer with the flat beater or a large bowl using a hand mixer, place the cornmeal, achiote paste, salt, and cumin and mix. Add the water and 6 tablespoons oil and mix until all the flour is moistened. Cover with a kitchen towel and set aside for 5 minutes. Mix again on low speed for 10 minutes.

5. On a workspace, place a 3-foot-long piece of plastic wrap. Divide the dough into 1½-inch balls and cover them with a kitchen towel while not being used. With a heavy pot, flatten each ball between 2 pieces of parchment paper into ⅛-inch-thick discs. Add a tablespoonful of filling to one side of the disc, cover with the other side, and cut with a coffee cup or cookie cutter (see note). Reuse leftover dough to make more empanadas.

6. Line a plate with paper towels. In a deep heavy pot over medium-high heat, add the oil and bring it to about 350° to 375°F. Deep-fry a few empanadas at a time for 2 to 3 minutes. The empanadas should feel crispy and hard on the outside. (They are not fully cooked if they stick to each other.) Remove them from the oil and place on the prepared plate to drain.

7. Serve with lime wedges and any of the ajíes in this book: The Magic Is Strong! Spicy Ají (page 26), Cilantro Pachanguero Salsa (page 28), Spice Lovers Peanut Ají (page 18), Uno, Dos, Tres Avocado Spread (page 31), or Gift Ceremony Tomato Salsa (page 29).

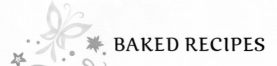
**Difficulty:** Medium Hard
**Prep time:** 20 minutes (plus 45 minutes resting)
**Cook time:** 10 minutes
**Yield:** 14 to 16 three-inch pastries | V

# Lunchbox Cheese Pastries
## *Deditos de queso*

Lunchbox Cheese Pastries are as tasty a treat for children as coffee is for grown-ups! The town kids in *Encanto* would surely have a fantastical day at school with cheesy pastries like these in their lunch boxes.

These *Deditos de queso* are made with farmer cheese wrapped in dough and baked to magical perfection, making them a delicious snack that even adults will enjoy with coffee or a refreshing drink.

2 cups flour, plus extra for rolling

2 teaspoons sugar

1½ teaspoons baking powder

1 teaspoon salt

6 tablespoons butter, cold

12 ounces white farmer cheese

1 egg white or yolk, lightly beaten, to brush on the dough

3 cups sunflower oil, if frying

1 oiled baking sheet, if baking

**NOTE:** The resting period is essential to make the dough easy to roll out without it shrinking back.

1. In a food processor, mix the flour, sugar, baking powder, and salt for 10 seconds. Add the cold butter and pulse 10 seconds more until the mixture is crumbly. Add ⅓ cup water and pulse for another 30 seconds or until the dough comes together, forms a ball, and pulls away from the sides of the bowl. Wrap the dough in plastic and refrigerate for 30 to 45 minutes to allow it to rest.

2. Cut the cheese into sticks that are ¼ inch thick and ⅓ inch wide, with a length of 2½ inches.

3. Sprinkle some flour over a work surface. With a rolling pin, roll the dough out to a rectangle about 16 by 12 inches. Cut into sixteen ½-inch-wide strips and brush the dough with the beaten egg. Wrap each strip around each piece of cheese and carefully press on the ends so that they are well sealed.

4. To bake: Preheat the oven to 475°F. Place the pastries on the prepared baking sheet and bake for about 15 minutes or until lightly golden.

5. To fry: Line a plate with paper towels. In a deep heavy pot over medium-high heat, add the oil and bring it to 350°F. Place the pastries one by one in the pot and fry for 30 to 40 seconds, turning them until lightly golden. Place on the prepared plate to drain and serve.

# Baked Cassava Bread
## *Pandebono*

When you must reroute the river, get the donkeys back in their stable, or tackle many chores as Luisa does in *Encanto*, it's important to remember to take a deep breath and have a little snack to fuel your energy.

*Pandebonos* are dough balls or ring-shaped doughs made from cassava flour and cheese that are then baked until they triple in size and fill your Casita with a delightful aroma. They can be made quickly and are a delicious, vegetarian, and naturally gluten-free alternative to bread.

Oil spray, for baking sheet

12 ounces hard white farmer cheese

½ cup cassava starch, yuca starch

¼ cup cassava starch, sour cassava

2 tablespoons precooked yellow cornmeal

1 tablespoon sugar

½ teaspoon salt

1 egg

**NOTE:** Before you form the pieces, make sure you followed the 2 minutes processing directions precisely (see step 1) for them to inflate properly! The mixture will leave the sides of the food processor soon after beginning to mix, but continue mixing for the 2 entire minutes. Stop and feel the dough. It should feel silky with no cheese crumbs to the touch.

The form you give these cassava breads does not matter, as long as they are not larger than 3 inches wide. If they are larger, the hole in the center will close and they might take a few minutes longer to cook.

1. Preheat the oven to 475°F. The oven must be very hot, so preheating is essential! Oil a baking sheet.

2. In a food processor, finely process the cheese. Add the cassava starches, cornmeal, sugar, and salt into the food processor and mix for 15 seconds. Add the egg and process 2 minutes more, or until you no longer feel the cheese when you rub a little between your fingers (see note).

3. On a workspace, place the dough and form ball, roll into a log and cut into 16 equal pieces. Roll each piece into about ⅓-inch-wide by 5-inch-long piece. Join the ends to form a teardrop shape. Place on the prepared baking sheet.

4. Place the baking sheet in the oven, close the oven door, and reduce the temperature to 425°F. Cook for 10 minutes or until lightly golden. Serve for breakfast or snack time with Heartwarming Cocoa Hug (page 159).

# Savory Sandy Cookies
## *Panderos*

These cookies are a powdery delight that dissolves in your mouth. Bruno would probably have a vision! Of you . . . indulging in one or two of these delicious cookies with your morning coffee.

*Panderos* are square-shaped biscuits with unique fingerprint-like patterns originating from Colombia's coffee-growing regions. Because of their special look, they're frequently included in gift baskets, like the "not special special" basket Don Osvaldo gives Mirabel before Antonio's gift ceremony.

5 tablespoons butter, plus more for greasing

1¾ cups cassava starch (sweet or plain) plus ¼ cup for rolling

⅓ cup granulated sugar

¼ cup raw sugar or panela

1 teaspoon baking powder

¼ teaspoon ground anise seed

⅛ teaspoon salt

1 egg

1. Preheat the oven to 350ºF. Grease two baking sheets with butter.

2. In a food processor, place the starch, sugar, raw sugar, baking powder, ground anise seed, and salt and mix for 10 seconds. Add the egg, butter, and 1 tablespoon water and mix on low speed for 30 seconds and high speed for 4 minutes.

3. Place parchment paper on your worktable, sprinkle some starch, and drop the dough. Cut into 3 pieces and roll each one into 1-inch-wide by 10-inch-long logs and press to flatten it into rectangles. Use the parchment to help with the rolling. If the dough sticks to the paper, add 1 tablespoon of cornstarch at a time and mix until the dough no longer sticks. Cut the long pieces of dough into 1-inch squares and mark each cookie with a fork or your finger by pressing on the center. Transfer to the prepared baking sheets.

4. Place the sheets in the oven and reduce the temperature to 325°F. Bake for 15 minutes or until the cookies look pale on top and lightly golden on the bottom. Set aside to cool and serve or store in airtight containers.

**Difficulty:** Medium
**Prep time:** 10 minutes | **Cook time:** 15 minutes
**Yield:** 8 to 12 empanadas

# Sunrise Beef Turnovers
## *Empanadas de carne*

Welcome to the land of half-moon-shaped pies with a crispy crust and a whimsical, flavorful, saucy meat and potato filling.

Describing empanadas could make every member of the Madrigal family's mouth water but making this recipe to enjoy for breakfast or as an afternoon snack will open all the magical doors in Casita and help you celebrate the taste of one of Colombia's best culinary staples.

These are best eaten with Heartwarming Cocoa Hug (page 159), Grown-Ups' Morning Boost (page 155), or a lemonade.

### For the filling

1 recipe of Familia's Sofrito (page 17)

1 pound ground beef

¼ cup stock, or ¼ cup water and ½ teaspoon bouillon base concentrate

¼ cup raisins

¼ cup minced cilantro

2 hard-boiled eggs

1 raw egg

### For the dough

2½ cups flour, plus extra for rolling

½ teaspoon baking powder

1 teaspoon salt

½ cup butter, chopped and cold (1 stick)

½ cup cold water

1 tablespoon vinegar

### Specialty Tools

3- to 4-inch round cookie cutters

1. To make the filling: Prepare the Familia's Sofrito in a large pan. Add the beef and stock to the pan and cook over medium heat until the beef is fully cooked, about 10 minutes. Add the raisins and cilantro, mix, and set aside to cool. The filling should be moist, not watery. (Transfer to a baking sheet so it cools faster.)

2. Peel and dice the hard-boiled eggs, add to the cool filling, and mix. Place the raw egg in a small bowl and whisk to use as an egg wash.

3. To make the dough: Place the flour, baking powder, and salt in a food processor and mix for 10 seconds. Add the cold butter and mix for 30 seconds more. Add the water and vinegar until you have a dough that separates from the sides of the processor (the dough can be a bit sticky). Transfer the dough to a large bowl, cover with plastic, and set aside for 30 minutes.

4. Preheat the oven to 325°F. Line a baking sheet with parchment paper.

5. Sprinkle flour on your workspace. Roll the dough and cut it into circles with 3- to 4-inch round cookie cutters. Add 1 tablespoon of filling in the center of each circle and brush the borders of the dough with egg wash. Fold the dough in half over the filling to create a half-moon shape and press with your fingers to close.

6. Place the empanadas on the prepared baking sheet and brush with the remaining egg wash. Bake for 20 to 25 minutes or until lightly golden. Serve warm.

**Difficulty:** Medium
**Prep time:** 35 minutes | **Cook time:** 5 minutes
**Yield:** 18 to 24 plantain balls
**GF, DF**

# Chunky Plantain Surprise Balls
## Marranitas

*Marranitas* are golf-ball-size treats made of mashed plantains and pork cracklings, forming freckled bites resembling the rolling mountains of Colombia in *Encanto*.

The mashed plantain gives these balls a fun lumpy texture, and as soon as you take a bite, you're surprised by the crunch of the crispy pork cracklings. But don't get distracted chewing if you hear loud cracks . . . it might be Casita magically encouraging you to save the miracle!

½ teaspoon beef or chicken bouillon base concentrate

3 cloves garlic, mashed

1 teaspoon salt

5 green plantains

4 cups sunflower oil, for frying

2 cups minced chicharrones from Famous Colombian Fried Pork Belly (page 85)

**Specialty Tools:**
Kitchen thermometer

1. In a small pot over medium heat, place 1 cup water, the bouillon base concentrate, garlic, and salt, and cook for 1 minute. Set aside.

2. Line a plate with paper towels. Peel the plantains. Slice each plantain into 3 or 4 pieces. In a deep pot over medium heat, bring the oil to 300°F. Add the plantain pieces and deep-fry for 10 to 12 minutes. The oil must cover the plantain pieces. They should barely simmer in the oil, and look dry on the outside, but not golden. When pressed they will be soft enough to be rolled. Remove the plantains from the oil with a slotted spoon and place on the prepared plate to drain.

3. Place a piece of parchment paper on a work surface and add a piece of drained plantain. Cover the plantain piece with another piece of parchment paper. With a heavy, flat-bottomed pot or a meat pounder, press the plantain until it becomes very thin (⅛ inch). Remove the top piece of parchment from the flattened plantain and place it (with the bottom piece of parchment) on the palm of your hand. Add ½ tablespoon of the chicharrones, and close your hand to form a ball, with the plantain covering the chicharrones. Press on all sides to make the plantain stick together tightly. Dunk the plantain ball into the bouillon water, press again, and set aside on a baking sheet.

4. Line a plate with paper towels. Increase the temperature of the oil to 350°F, and fry the filled balls for about 4 minutes, or until lightly golden. Remove from the oil, place on the prepared plate to drain, and serve.

Chapter

3

# Soups
# and Stews

**Difficulty:** Medium
**Prep time:** 1 hour | **Cook time:** 1½ hours
**Yield:** 10 to 12 servings
**GF**

# Miracle and Love Celebration Soup
## *Ajiaco bogotano*

Most Latin families love celebrations! When we're not moving to the beat of cumbia and vallenato music, we're doing the next best thing—bonding over the joy of sharing food during festive moments.

Gathered around Casita's table with the Guzmáns, the Madrigals celebrate Isa and Mariano's possible engagement with a feast. The dishes passed around that night, such as white rice, avocados, corn, and cream, are traditionally served with ajiaco, a wholesome soup from Colombia's capital, Bogotá.

### For the stock:

1 pound beef bones or oxtail

2 whole ears of corn (not sweet), sliced in half

½ cup cilantro

2 teaspoons freshly-ground black pepper

### For the chicken and potatoes:

4 skinned, bone-in chicken breasts

½ ounce dry guascas, gallant soldier herb (about ¾ cup fresh) (see page 12)

4 whole green onions, white and green parts (about 1½ cups)

2 cloves garlic

1 tablespoon salt

12 small russet potatoes, peeled and sliced 3 to 4 inches long (about 3 cups)

12 small red potatoes, peeled and sliced 1 to 2 inches long (about 3 cups)

18 medium peeled and 1- to 2-inch-long sliced papas criollas, yellow Peruvian potatoes, or yellow fingerling potatoes (about 5 cups)

Salt and freshly-ground black pepper, to taste

### For serving:

2 pounds cooked Candlelight White Rice (see page 107), for serving

1½ cups heavy cream, for serving

3 to 4 avocados, quartered, for serving

1 cup capers, for serving

1. To make the stock: Place the beef bones and corn in a pressure cooker with ¼ cup cilantro and the freshly-ground black pepper. Cover with water and cook for 50 minutes. Remove the beef and corn, set aside, and keep the stock.

2. To make the chicken and potatoes: In a large stockpot over medium-high heat, place 10 cups water, the chicken breasts, guascas, green onions, garlic, and salt. Bring to a boil, reduce the heat to low, cover, and simmer for 20 minutes. Remove the chicken, shred it, and set aside. Add the russet, red, and yellow potatoes, and the reserved beef stock to the stockpot and simmer for 1 hour.

3. If the soup looks clear like stock, blend 4 to 6 of the yellow potatoes or use an immersion blender for 10 seconds to blend some of the potatoes and thicken the soup a little. Season with salt and freshly-ground black pepper to taste.

4. To serve: Serve with the corn, shredded chicken, and remaining ¼ cup minced cilantro on top. On the side, serve white rice, cream, avocado, and capers.

5. *Ajiaco* is a presentation event: the soup is served in a large bowl, and the rest of the ingredients are served as sides to pass around.

**Difficulty:** Easy
**Prep time:** 1 hour | **Cook time:** 2 hours
**Yield:** 12 servings
**GF**

# Fiesta en el Valle Chicken Soup
## *Sancocho valluno*

When Abuela finds Mirabel by the river in *Encanto*, she finally sees the true magic in the miracle she's given and realizes that grandiose powers are not always the most important when simple but meaningful things can also be a real gift.

One of the many humble but significant traditions loved and preserved in Colombia's Valle del Cauca is planning a Sunday trip with family and friends to the Pance River. A huge pot sits over a log fire from very early in the morning until the afternoon when, after a whole day of music, laughter, and games, a magical soup carefully crafted with wholesome ingredients and love is ready for everyone to enjoy.

**For the soup:**

1 pound chicken wings

2 fresh corncobs, cut into 4 pieces

1 bunch cilantro

4 whole scallions

4 leaves cimarron or cilantro (spiny cilantro)

1 tablespoon minced garlic

1 tablespoon chicken bouillon concentrate base

1 tablespoon salt

1 teaspoon freshly-ground black pepper

12 chicken breasts or 3 whole chickens, skinned (keep the bones if possible for the soup) and cut into serving pieces

3 peeled green plantains, halved lengthwise and cut into 1½-inch pieces

2 pounds peeled yuca, quartered lengthwise and cut into 2-inch pieces

12 small potatoes, peeled and halved lengthwise

1 recipe Familia's Sofrito (page 17)

**For the sides:**

¼ cup minced cilantro leaves

6 cups Candlelight White Rice (page 107)

3 avocados, quartered

1. In a large pot over medium-high heat, tie the chicken wings and the chicken bones, if available, (tied together in cheesecloth), the corn, 10 cilantro sprigs with stems, the scallions, cimarron, garlic, bouillon base concentrate, salt, and freshly-ground black pepper. Add 4 quarts water, bring to a boil, cover, and cook for 30 minutes.

2. Add the chicken breasts or pieces, and simmer for 30 minutes. Remove the chicken breasts and set aside onto a plate. Add the plantains, yuca, and potatoes, and simmer for 45 minutes more. Remove the bones and wings in the cheesecloth.

3. Add Familia's Sofrito to the pot, cover, and simmer for 15 minutes. Serve the clear soup in a pot and the yuca, chicken, corn, and plantain over the soup. On a side plate, place a piece of the chicken, Candlelight White Rice, avocado, and Baked Sweet Plantain Boats (page 130) and serve with Cilantro Pachanguero Salsa (page 28). Place the minced cilantro in a small bowl for garnishing the soup.

**Difficulty:** Easy
**Prep time:** 10 minutes | **Cook time:** 15 minutes
**Yield:** 4 servings
**GF, V**

# Lazy Sunday Cloudy Egg Soup
## *Changua*

Sundays are perfect for resting and preparing simple meals that are easy to make and enjoy. Camilo might use his gift so a mother can nap while her baby is cared for, and Luisa might sit back and relax in a hammock while Tía Pepa happily sways under a sky of worry-free fluffy clouds.

This Cloudy Egg Soup is our version of *Changua* and is the perfect recipe for a stress-free day. Just like breakfast could be enjoyed at any time of the day, soup is often served for breakfast in Colombia, particularly in the Andean region, where low temperatures are common throughout the year.

2 cups milk

1 garlic clove, minced

2 scallions, thinly sliced

½ cup finely chopped cilantro

¼ teaspoon salt

¼ teaspoon freshly-ground black pepper

4 eggs

4 slices of toast

1. Place 4 cups of water and the milk in a small pot, and add the garlic, half of the scallions, and half of the cilantro. Season with the salt and freshly-ground black pepper. Place on high heat and bring to a boil, then reduce the heat to low and simmer for 10 minutes. Strain the liquid into a bowl through a sieve and return the liquid to the pan. Discard the solids and increase the heat to medium.

2. Once the soup comes to a simmer, crack the eggs one by one into a small cup and gently slide them into the hot liquid to poach. The soup is then stirred, so the important part is that the yolk stays whole. Cook for 4 minutes (or poach each egg separately) and transfer one egg into each of four serving cups. Sprinkle each with the remaining scallions and cilantro. Pour the hot soup over the eggs and serve immediately with the toast.

**Difficulty:** Easy
**Prep time:** 1 hour | **Cook time:** 2½ hours
**Yield:** 8 servings
**GF, V**

# Yummy Cheesy Yam Soup
## *Mote de queso*

With its African-inherited name, which means "to eat," *ñame*, or yam, is widely used in recipes around the world. This type of root vegetable thrives in the warm, starry evenings of tropical towns such as the magical one in *Encanto*.

One of our favorite yam recipes is called *Mote de queso*. This soup is a creamy and delicious concoction that will warm your soul as you taste the oozing cheese with every spoonful. So yummy!

5 pounds tropical hairy or cheeky yams (about 3 yams)(see note)

3 to 4 teaspoons salt

1 tablespoon chicken or vegetable bouillon base concentrate

2 cups Familia's Sofrito (about 2 recipes' worth) (page 17)

2 pounds white farmer cheese, cut in ¼-inch dice

1 recipe Candlelight White Rice (page 107)

2 large avocados or 4 Hass avocados

1 recipe Charming Sauce (page 19)

1. Peel the cheeky yams. Cut lengthwise, then into strips, and then into 2-inch chunks. In a large stockpot over medium-high heat, place half the yams and cover with 12 cups water, 2 teaspoons of the salt, and the bouillon base concentrate. Once it simmers, cover, lower the heat to medium, and cook for 1 hour. Add the remaining cheeky yams and continue to cook for another hour.

2. When the cheeky yam has cooked through and the soup has thickened and turned white, pour in the Familia's Sofrito, mix, and cook for 10 minutes. Add the cheese and simmer for 10 minutes more and serve hot. Taste for salt and add the remaining 1 to 2 teaspoons, if needed.

3. Serve with the Candlelight White Rice, avocados, and Charming Sauce.

**NOTE:** It's best to use yellow yams with white flesh in order to achieve the classic creamy look of this recipe; using orange, red, or purple yams will yield the reddish hue shown here.

**Difficulty:** Easy

**Prep time:** 1 hour plus 2 hours | **Cook time:** 3½ hours

**Yield:** 12 servings

**GF**

# Magical Vision Soup
## *Sancocho trifásico*

To prepare for a busy day of lifting churches with Luisa or spinning sand for a clairvoyance session with Tío Bruno, you need a nourishing meal that provides strength and happiness.

*Sancocho trifásico* is made by simmering an extensive assortment of ingredients and combining them with the essence of hard work, community, and gratitude. All these flavors are transformed into a soup so memorable and energizing it'll give you the strength to help the Madrigals rebuild Casita!

### For the soup:

6 scallions, chopped, white and green parts

6 green ajíes dulces (sweet peppers), seeded and chopped (about ½ cup)

3 cloves garlic

3 carrots, chopped

2 medium yellow onions, chopped

2 celery stalks, chopped

1 cup chopped flat kale

1 teaspoon freshly-ground black pepper

3 teaspoons achiote paste or 1½ teaspoons turmeric

½ teaspoon allspice

½ teaspoon ground cumin

3 pounds short beef brisket, cut into 1½-inch pieces

3 pounds pork ham hock, cut into pieces

2 whole chickens, skinned and cut into serving pieces

3 tablespoon olive oil

3 corncobs, each cut into 4 pieces

1½ tablespoons salt

1¼ pounds cassava, peeled and cut into 2-inch pieces

1 pound pumpkin, peeled and cut into 2-inch chunks

1 green plantain, peeled and cut into 6 pieces

1 pound cheeky yams, cut into 2-inch pieces

1½ pounds red russet potatoes, peeled and halved

1¼ pounds yams, peeled and cut into 2-inch chunks (about 1 yam)

1 cup chopped cilantro leaves (about 1 bunch)

½ tablespoon lime juice

2 ripe plantains, ends cut and unpeeled, cut into 6 pieces

### For serving:

2 scallions, thinly sliced, white and green parts

3 tablespoons minced cilantro

6 cups Candlelight White Rice (page 107)

6 limes, sliced

1. In a food processor, add the scallions, ajíes dulces, and garlic and process to a fine grind. Add the carrots, onions, celery, kale, freshly-ground black pepper, 2 teaspoons of the achiote paste or 1 teaspoon of the turmeric, the allspice, and cumin and process for 1 minute. Rub over the beef, pork, and chicken pieces and set aside for 2 hours.

2. In a large stockpot, place the oil, the remaining 1 teaspoon achiote paste or ½ teaspoon turmeric, and all the meats and cook for 5 minutes per side until golden brown, about 30 minutes. Add 10 quarts water and the corn, cover, and simmer for 30 minutes. Add the salt, mix, remove the chicken and set aside, and continue to cook the soup for another hour. Add the cassava, pumpkin, and green plantains to the pot and cook 30 minutes. Add the cheeky yams, potatoes, yam, and cilantro, and cook covered for 45 minutes until the beef and pork bone meats are fork tender.

3. In a medium pot, simmer the remaining 4 cups water with 1 teaspoon of the lime juice, and add the sweet plantains (with skin). Cook for 30 minutes, then set the pot aside.

4. Serve the clear soup in a pot, and the meat, roots, and tubers on different platters. Add the scallions and cilantro on top of the soup. The white rice, lime slices, and sweet plantain chunks are served on other platters.

5. Serve with The Magic Is Strong! Spicy Ají (page 26), Cilantro Pachanguero Salsa (page 28), or Open Door House Salad (page 32).

# Enchanting Coconut Seafood Chowder
## *Cazuela de mariscos al coco*

**Difficulty:** Easy
**Prep time:** 1 hour | **Cook time:** 1 hour
**Yield:** 6 to 8 servings
**GF**

Colombia's Pacific region is known for its bountiful seafood and cultural diversity. Traditional food is prepared for large celebrations as the sun sets over the ocean, while the sounds of marimbas become one with the chants of the waves.

Just as magical as when Antonio timidly touches his doorknob, and everyone watches the sparkling door open to reveal the endless details of the youngest Madrigal's rainforest room, this Enchanting Coconut Seafood Chowder will open your senses to realize that magic can also come in the form of delicious food.

### For the seafood seasoning:

1½ pounds raw shrimp, clean and deveined

½ pound raw squid rings, cleaned

½ pound clams, cleaned

2 tablespoons olive oil

¼ cup minced cilantro

¼ cup minced parsley

1 pound prawns or jumbo shrimp, clean and deveined (about 8)

8 mussels on their shell

### For the chowder:

2 tablespoons olive oil

2 tablespoons garlic paste

1 cup grated onion (about 1 onion)

1 cup grated red bell pepper (about 1 bell pepper)

1 tablespoon fish bouillon base concentrate

1¼ teaspoons salt

½ teaspoon cumin

½ teaspoon achiote paste or ¼ teaspoon turmeric

¾ teaspoon freshly-ground black pepper

4 cups coconut milk (freshly made, see page 23)

2 cups milk (dairy, oat, or other)

4 tablespoons cornstarch

¼ cup white wine

¼ cup minced parsley or cilantro, for serving

3 sliced lemons, for serving

1 recipe Dazzling White Coconut Rice (page 106)

1 recipe Sweet Plantain Wedges (page 129)

**NOTES:** You can use a 2½- to 3-pound bag of mixed seafood in place of all the individual ingredients.

Using a wide pot rather than a deep one is recommended for best results.

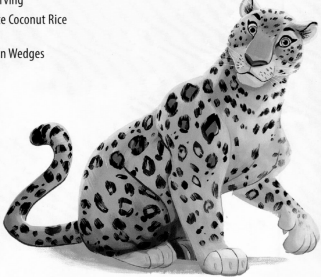

1. To season the seafood: In a large bowl, add the shrimp, squid rings, clams, 1 tablespoon of the olive oil, 2 tablespoons of the cilantro, and 2 tablespoons of the parsley. Mix and refrigerate. In a second large bowl add the prawns, mussels, and the remaining 1 tablespoon olive oil, 2 tablespoons cilantro, and 2 tablespoons parsley, mix, and also refrigerate.

2. To make the chowder: In a large, wide heavy pot or caldero over medium-low heat, place the olive oil, garlic, onion, red bell pepper, bouillon base concentrate, salt, cumin, achiote paste, and freshly-ground black pepper, and sauté for 3 minutes.

3. In a medium bowl, mix the cool coconut milk, 2 cups water (3 cups if using canned coconut milk), milk (or alternative), and cornstarch together to a smooth consistency. Add the squid, shrimp, clams, and the milk mixture to the pot. Simmer over low heat for 20 minutes. Add the wine and the prawns and mussels mixture and simmer for 15 minutes.

4. Remove most shrimp and mussels from the cooked soup for serving and set aside. Pour the soup into bowls and place the shrimp and mussels on top. Sprinkle some parsley or cilantro and serve lemon slices on the side. Dazzling White Coconut Rice (page 106) and Sweet Plantain Wedges (page 129) are served as sides, but the soup can be a dish on its own and served with an Open Door House Salad (page 32).

Chapter

# 4

# Pork, Beef, and Poultry

**Difficulty:** Difficult
**Prep time:** 1½ hours | **Cook time:** 1½ hours
**Yield:** 8 servings
**GF, DF**

# Paisa Family Platter
## *Bandeja paisa*

Many of Colombia's natural, cultural, and culinary gifts come from Antioquia's lively and mountainous region, where people are called paisas.

Bandeja paisa may seem complex to prepare, but it's a delightful dish that captures the rich flavors of Colombia. It's a popular comfort food for family gatherings, like the Madrigal primos' celebration after a long day of sharing their magical gifts with the community.

1 recipe Magic Doorknob Meat Powder (page 74)

1 recipe Did Someone Say Beans? (page 120)

1 recipe Charming Sauce (page 19)

1 recipe Famous Colombian Fried Pork Belly (page 85)

8 small chorizos

1 recipe Sweet Plantain Wedges (page 129)

8 eggs

2 cups Candlelight White Rice (page 107)

1. Prepare the Magic Doorknob Meat Powder, Did Someone Say Beans?, and Charming Sauce in advance (this can be done the day before). Prepare the Famous Colombian Fried Pork Belly and the Candlelight White Rice about one hour before serving.

2. To prepare the chorizos, prick them with a fork, then make cuts on the bias (so they cook faster). In a large, heavy pan over medium heat, place the chorizos, cook for 2 minutes and turn, cooking all sides in about 8 minutes. If your pan is not large enough to fit all the chorizos, cook in two batches.

3. About 15 minutes before serving, fry the Sweet Plantain Wedges and place them on paper towels to drain. Fry the eggs (one will be served on each plate) and set aside.

4. Mold the Candlelight White Rice into eight coffee cups, and place one cup in the center of each platter. Add a ladle of Did Someone Say Beans? and a ladle of Magic Doorknob Meat Powder. Around the sides of the platter, arrange the cooked chorizos, Famous Colombian Fried Pork Belly, and Sweet Plantain Wedges. Over the beans, place a fried egg. Serve Charming Sauce on the side.

**Difficulty:** Easy
**Prep time:** 15 minutes | **Cook time:** 10 minutes
**Yield:** 6 to 8 servings
**GF, DF**

# Magic Doorknob Meat Powder
## *Carne en polvo*

The magic in Casita's doors comes to life with a simple touch from its wielder's hand. Glowing doorknobs and sparkles anticipate the arrival of a magical gift.

Food is a magical part of our lives that ignites excitement and anticipation. And, just like the sparkles of these doorknobs, our *Carne en polvo* has the power of creating and complementing a variety of meals.

It is made by cooking ground beef and "pulverizing" it until the beef turns into a powder-like texture that enhances the flavors of anything that is sprinkled or mixed with it.

2 pounds beef flank or skirt steak, diced into 1-inch pieces

½ cup grainy mustard

½ cup chopped scallions, white and green parts

½ cup chopped yellow onion (about ½ onion)

3 cloves garlic

¼ teaspoon freshly-ground black pepper

½ teaspoon salt

1. In the bowl of a pressure cooker, place the beef pieces and rub them with the mustard. Add the scallions, onion, garlic, freshly-ground black pepper, and 1 cup water to the bottom of the pot.

2. Pressure-cook the beef for 50 minutes. After cooking, remove the beef from the pressure cooker and place it on a baking sheet to rapidly cool to room temperature, about 10 minutes. Save the cooking liquid for use in other recipes like Did Someone Say Beans? (page 120) or Colombian Power Lentils (refer to page 116).

3. Transfer the beef to a food processor, add the salt, and process into a powder-like consistency.

4. Add to dishes like Did Someone Say Beans? (page 120), Candlelight White Rice (page 107), Paisa Family Platter (page 73), Colombian Power Lentils (page 116), Sweet Plantain Wedges (page 129), or Gift Ceremony Tomato Salsa (page 29).

**Difficulty:** Easy
**Prep time:** 30 minutes | **Cook time:** 1 hour
**Yield:** 6 servings
**GF, DF**

# Amazing Shredded Beef
## *Carne desmechada*

Treat your taste buds to an amazing experience with this flavor-packed dish featuring pulled beef smothered in a luscious peppery sauce.

With roots in the Spanish and indigenous culinary traditions, our Amazing Shredded Beef, or *Carne desmechada*, recipe can feature long, tender shreds or bite-size pieces.

*Carne desmechada's* versatility is what makes it so magical! It can be enjoyed as a main course, used as a filling in arepas or empanadas, or served as a topping with rice and pasta.

2 pounds beef skirt steak in one piece

½ cup grainy mustard

1 cup grated red bell pepper (about 1 bell pepper)

2 carrots, grated

3 cloves garlic, minced

2 recipes Familia's Sofrito (page 17) (about 2 cups)

2 tablespoons butter or olive oil

2 whole eggs (optional)

**NOTE:** You can process the red bell pepper, carrots, garlic, and mustard and then rub onto the beef, if desired.

1. In the bowl of a pressure cooker, place the beef and rub with the mustard. Add the bell pepper, carrots, and garlic, and set aside for 10 minutes or more.

2. Pressure cook for 50 minutes. You know the meat is done when you can shred it easily with a fork. Remove the beef and place on a baking pan to shred. Return the bowl with the cooking liquid to the pressure cooker and, on sauté, cook for 5 to 8 minutes or until the cooking liquid has thickened to a sauce and reduced to about 1 cup.

3. Shred the meat with 2 forks, add half of the Familia's Sofrito, mix, return the beef to the pressure cooker pot, and mix with the thickened sauce.

4. If eggs are used, in a small pan over medium-high heat, add the butter or olive oil, spread it on the pan, and then crack the two eggs into the pan. With a mixing spoon, mix the eggs while they cook to break them up. Add them to the beef and mix.

5. Serve with the remaining half of the Familia's Sofrito over the beef or on the side.

6. Serve with Candlelight White Rice (page 107), or Moonlight Baked Yellow Potatoes (page 118), Did Someone Say Beans? (page 120), Colombian Power Lentils (page 116), Sweet Plantain Wedges (page 129), Gift Ceremony Tomato Salsa (page 29), or Baked Sweet Plantain Boats (page 130).

**Difficulty:** Medium
**Prep time:** 30 minutes | **Cook time:** 10 minutes
**Yield:** 6 servings
**GF**

# Beef Fillet with Golden Onions
## *Bistec encebollado*

Transport yourself to a golden afternoon in the town of *Encanto* with this delightful sauce. Infused with sautéed onions, cognac, and spices, it adds a burst of flavor to a succulent beef fillet.

*Bistec encebollado* is a delicious dish traditionally using beef fillet, but skirt steak can be a great alternative. Our variation of this classic recipe involves cooking 1½-inch-sliced beef fillet to medium wellness, resulting in juicy and tender meat that perfectly complements the rich and flavorful golden onion sauce. As with many of our dishes, this one reflects the exciting and diverse influences of Middle Eastern and European cuisines in Colombian cooking.

3 pounds fillet of beef, cut into 1½-inch-thick steaks

1 clove garlic, minced

1 tablespoon mustard

¼ teaspoon freshly-ground black pepper

1 tablespoon olive oil

1 teaspoon salt

2 tablespoons cognac or brandy

2 tablespoons butter

Enchanting Colombia Onion Sauce (page 20)

1. In a large bowl, place the beef, add the garlic, mustard, and freshly-ground black pepper, and rub the mixture over the beef.

2. In a large skillet heat the oil over medium-high heat, add the beef, and cook for 3 minutes on each side for medium rare, 4 minutes for medium, and 5 minutes for well done. Cook them in two batches, making sure the steaks do not touch in the skillet. Add the salt while cooking. Remove the steaks from the skillet. Add the cognac and butter to the skillet and mix. Add the Enchanting Colombia Onion Sauce to the skillet, mix again, and serve over each steak.

3. Serve with Candlelight White Rice (page 107) and Open Door House Salad (page 32).

**Difficulty:** Medium
**Prep time:** 30 minutes | **Cook time:** 10 minutes
**Yield:** 6 servings
**GF, DF**

# Townspeople Creole Steak
## Bistec a la criolla

Casita's table might be set for a mouthwatering meal that is sure to impress everyone in town. Get ready to feast and witness dancing plates and sparkling creole flavors!

The savory beef, infused with a flavorful tomato sauce, evokes our African heritage ingrained in Colombia's local cuisine and music, forever alive in *Encanto*'s vibrant community. Serve it on top of Candlelight White Rice (page 107) and with a side of Open Door House Salad (page 32) to create a magical feast that will satisfy a large group of guests like the Madrigals and the townspeople from the village in *Encanto*!

1 recipe To the Rhythm of the Creole Sauce (page 22)

1 tablespoon sunflower oil

3 cloves garlic, minced

½ teaspoon freshly-ground black pepper

2 pounds beef sirloin or flank steak, thinly sliced

1 teaspoon salt

¼ cup cilantro, chopped

1. Make the To the Rhythm of the Creole Sauce.
2. In a large bowl, mix the oil, garlic, and freshly-ground black pepper, and spread over each slice of meat.
3. In a large skillet over medium-high heat, space each piece of meat so they are not touching. This allows them to brown evenly and can be done in batches. Cook the beef on both sides: cook 2 minutes (rare), 4 minutes (medium), or 6 minutes (well done). Sprinkle the salt over the beef and transfer to a serving platter.
4. Pour the To the Rhythm of the Creole Sauce into the pan's beef drippings, scrape the pan, add the cilantro to the skillet, and stir to combine. Pour the sauce over the steaks and serve immediately with rice or Behind the Walls Corn Arepas (page 37).

**NOTE:** To make the experience even more enjoyable, consider playing lively music and dancing while cooking.

**Difficulty:** Medium
**Prep time:** 30 minutes plus overnight resting time
**Cook time:** 45 minutes to 2 hours and 45 minutes
**Yield:** 6 to 8 servings | **GF, DF**

# Magical Sauce Beef Roast
## *Carne en posta*

This cut of beef roast, called *Carne en posta,* is served with a delicious sauce infused with burgundy wine, but for a kid-friendly twist, you can easily substitute the wine with dark soda or root beer. *Carne en posta* is a traditional dish from Cartagena de Indias, served at homes and elegant events too.

With every step, the rows of roses Isabela grows resemble the red-purple color of the silky sauce, which gets its hue from the burgundy wine. Trace the path of the jacarandas to the table, where you'll find the *Carne en posta* expertly sliced with a razor-sharp knife, creating delicate, thin pieces.

¼ cup mustard

½ cup minced scallions, white and green parts (about 2 scallions)

⅓ cup coconut aminos

2 teaspoons achiote paste or 1 teaspoon turmeric

6 cloves garlic

½ teaspoon freshly-ground black pepper

3 pounds beef rolled rump, eye of round, or top round, in 1 piece, some of the fat removed

1 recipe Familia's Sofrito (page 17)

2 tablespoons sunflower oil

1 red onion, quartered

⅓ cup tomato paste

⅓ cup brown sugar

¾ cup red wine, burgundy

2 teaspoons beef bouillon base concentrate

2 teaspoons salt

**NOTES:** In many parts of Colombia, regular cola soft drink is used instead of wine. Ketchup is also often used instead of tomato paste.

If the sauce from the cooking process is too thin, boil it down to a thicker sauce that still flows. If it's too dry from the oven, add some stock.

1. In a medium bowl, mix the mustard, scallion, coconut aminos, achiote paste, 3 pressed garlic cloves, and the freshly-ground black pepper and rub over the beef (with gloves as achiote stains red). Refrigerate overnight.

2. Remove the beef from the refrigerator and allow it to return to room temperature for about 30 minutes.

3. Prepare the Familia's Sofrito.

4. Preheat the oven to 425°F.

5. In a large heavy skillet or on a griddle heat the oil over medium-high heat, place the meat fat-side-down on the skillet, and cook for 7 to 9 minutes until most of the fat has rendered and browned. Turn on all other sides for 1 to 2 minutes until all sides are browned.

6. In an ovenproof pot with a lid, place the onion. In a medium bowl, mix the tomato paste, brown sugar, wine, bouillon base concentrate, remaining 3 garlic cloves, and salt, and pour over the browned beef. Cover the pot and cook in the oven for 30 minutes for rare or 45 minutes for medium. For well done, bake at 300°F for 2½ hours.

7. Remove the beef from the pot, place it on a pan, cover, and set aside for 10 minutes or more.

8. In a large bowl with a sieve, pour the drippings and vegetables from the pot. Pass through the sieve and place the solid ingredients from the sieve back into the cooking pot. Defat the sauce by pouring the liquid into a fat separator (a measuring cup with the spout in the bottom), letting the cup stand for 1 or 2 minutes so the fat floats upward, and pouring the bottom liquid carefully back into the pot. Repeat as necessary. Discard the remaining fat on the bottom of the cup. Mix the sauce in the pot with the cooked vegetables.

9. Slice the beef thinly and serve with the chunky sauce, dark coconut rice, sweet or savory plantains, and a nice drink.

**Difficulty:** Hard
**Prep time:** 20 minutes | **Cook time:** 20 minutes
**Yield:** Twelve 1½-inch sausages (6 servings)
**GF, DF**

# Firecracker Festival Beef and Pork Links
## *Butifarras*

These one-inch sausages are bursting with the explosive flavors of the Colombian Caribbean coast, infused with a fiery kick and the region's rich cultural traditions.

Firecracker Festival Beef and Pork Links, popularly known as butifarras, are a perfect blend of beef, pork, and a hint of pepper and spice, accompanied by refreshing lime slices. They are a must-have during the lively carnivals and festivals in Colombia's small towns like the one in Encanto, where street vendors prepare them fresh on their carts, catering to families who relish the sizzling delicacy.

4 cloves garlic

1½ teaspoons salt, plus extra for cooking

1½ teaspoons freshly-ground black pepper

¼ teaspoon ground cumin

1 pound flank steak, cubed

5 ounces pork belly that contains meat (not all fat), cubed

Pork casings, cleaned and ready to use

1. In a food processor, add the garlic, salt, freshly-ground black pepper, and cumin and process for 1 minute. Add the steak and pork belly and process to a paste. (If using a meat grinder, mix the meats after they are ground to ensure garlic and seasonings are well distributed within them.) Stuff the pork casings with the mixture.

2. In a large pot over high heat, bring 6 cups water and 1 tablespoon salt to a boil. Add the sausages and cook for 15 minutes. They should feel like they spring back when touched. Remove from the pot, set aside on a plate, and serve at room temperature or store in your refrigerator overnight. Serve them cold or hot.

3. To serve warm, grill, steam, or air fry 3 to 5 minutes or until the center is warm. Serve whole or sliced. Pair them with Behind the Walls Corn Arepas (page 37) or get creative and thread these zesty links onto skewers, transforming them into flavorful kabobs that will light up any gathering.

**Difficulty:** Easy
**Prep time:** 30 minutes | **Cook time:** 20 minutes
**Yield:** 6 to 8 servings
**GF, DF**

# Golden Chicken Stew
## *Pollo sudado*

A joyful and hassle-free meal that's served in a bowl, our Golden Chicken Stew is a savory and juicy dish that's topped with rice to upscale its magical taste.

*Pollo sudado* perfectly combines flavors from Colombia's mountains and plains, featuring tasty yellow potatoes seasoned with tropical spices. This recipe is a perfect one-pot wonder that would quickly satisfy the Madrigal family's cravings and put Pepa in her happiest mood!

1 tablespoon olive oil

½ teaspoon achiote paste or ¼ teaspoon turmeric

4 cloves garlic, mashed

1 teaspoon salt

½ teaspoon freshly-ground black pepper

6 chicken thighs (about 2 pounds)

1 cup chicken stock (or 1 cup water and 1 teaspoon bouillon base concentrate)

2 pounds yellow potatoes (about 10 potatoes)

2 large yellow onions, chopped (about 2 cups)

1 red bell pepper, chopped

1 cup chopped and seeded Roma tomatoes (about 2 tomatoes)

¼ cup minced cilantro

**NOTE:** If the liquid from the pressure cooker is watery, remove the chicken and boil it down to a sauce that still flows. If it is too dry, add some stock.

1. Place the olive oil, achiote paste, garlic, salt, and freshly-ground black pepper in the pot of a pressure cooker and sauté for 1 minute. Add the chicken, stock, potatoes, onions, bell pepper, tomatoes, and half of the cilantro. Cook covered under pressure for 15 minutes and serve with the remaining cilantro on top, Candlelight White Rice (page 107), and sweet plantains.

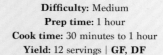

**Difficulty:** Medium
**Prep time:** 1 hour
**Cook time:** 30 minutes to 1 hour
**Yield:** 12 servings | **GF, DF**

# Famous Colombian Fried Pork Belly
## *Chicharrones*

Chicharrones, renowned both within and beyond Colombia, hold a cherished and unique spot in the hearts of people throughout the country.

Shape-shifted into perfectly crispy and crunchy fritters, these pork belly treats are truly magical. You'll find them in various sizes and shapes, ranging from tiny ¼-inch squares to generously long pieces that can barely fit on your plate.

Chicharrones are so tempting that even Camilo would be unable to resist using his gift to grab multiple servings.

3 pounds piece of pork belly or ribs with pork meat in them

1 tablespoon baking soda

1 teaspoon salt

**NOTE:** If using ribs, save the bones to cook in a pot with red beans. It is very traditional too.

1. Preheat the oven to 375°F. Line a rimmed baking sheet with parchment paper or a silicone baking mat. Line a second baking sheet with paper towels.

2. Place the pork on a cutting board, fat side down, and slice it into ½-inch strips. These strips serve as the basic width for the chicharrones. Next, you have the flexibility to cut the strips into desired sizes (cubes), and lengths. Finally, if desired, make vertical cuts on your long chicharrones to create fan-like shapes.

3. Rub the baking soda and salt over all the pork pieces and place them in a pan and set aside for 1 hour. Wash the pork pieces gently but well, with plenty of water. Place onto the first prepared baking sheet.

4. In the oven, cook the pork for 30 minutes to 1 hour depending on the size, or, until the fat has rendered out and you have crispy pieces of pork.

5. Place the pork on the second prepared baking sheet to remove any excess fat and serve warm or at room temperature alongside popular Colombian dishes like Paisa Family Platter (page 73) in slim 3-to-4-inch-long strips. On sides such as beans, lentils, arepas, or plantains, they are served in small 2-by-½-inch pieces or in crumbles. They complement a wide range of Colombian fare.

**Difficulty:** Hard
**Prep time:** 2 hours to 2 days | **Cook time:** 2½ to 3½ hours
**Yield:** 12 servings
GF, DF

# Pig in a Bag
## *Lechona en bolsa*

Pig in a Bag, or *Lechona en bolsa*, is a delicious, shortcut version of a traditional slow-cooked whole pork. Packed with mouthwatering flavors of roasted pork, rice, peas, potatoes, achiote, and Charming Sauce (page 19), this enthralling pork-stuffed dish is guaranteed to satisfy your taste buds.

Colombian families prepare this recipe in advance as it requires two days to complete. This way, it can be easily filled and cooked on the day of your celebration. Looking for a fantastic and perfect pairing? Serve with Hidden Egg Arepas (page 39)!

1 whole pork skin, cleaned, ½-inch thick, squared, and large enough to cut into an 18-by-24-inch rectangle (see note)

1 teaspoon baking soda

### Pork Meat and Seasoning

3 recipes of Charming Sauce (page 19)

3 pounds pork, cut into ½-inch dice

3 blood oranges, halved

5 cups Candlelight White Rice (page 107)

5 cups raw ½-inch diced red potatoes, cooked

2 cups green peas, cooked

½ cup chopped scallions

### Day 1

1. Remove the excess fat inside the pork skin with a sharp knife. Rub baking soda all over the pork skin, inside and out. Refrigerate covered for at least one hour or overnight.

2. Make the 3 batches of Charming Sauce all in one pot. Transfer to a baking pan and spread to cool quicker. Set aside 1 cup and refrigerate the rest covered overnight.

3. Take the 1 cup of Charming Sauce you set aside and mix it with the pork pieces in a large bowl; refrigerate them covered overnight.

### Day 2

4. Preheat the oven to 300°F.

5. Wash the pork skin well to remove all the baking soda. In a large pot of boiling water over medium-high heat, place the pork skin, and cook it until it has softened and is easier to bend, about 20 to 30 minutes. Remove from the pot and set aside on a plate until cool enough to handle.

6. Fold the skin in half and sew the two short sides together with a large needle and butcher's twine. We are forming an envelope-type rectangle with one opening. Place the skin on a large baking pan and rub the inside and outside of the sewn skin-bag with the blood orange halves. Set the blood orange halves in a bowl for later use.

7. Remove the seasoned pork pieces from the refrigerator and set aside.

8. Take the sewn skin of pork (the pork bag) and brush the inside with 1 cup of the refrigerated Charming Sauce. Lay the seasoned pork bag on the side, with the slit facing you, and begin to stuff it, keeping it as flat as possible (see note).

9. To fill the pork skin bag: First add the rice, then cover with the potatoes, and on top, lay the peas. Mix the pork with the leftover Charming Sauce and place in the bag. Sprinkle the scallions on top of the diced pork and tie the bag closed with more butcher's twine. Rub the bag all over with the blood oranges set aside in a bowl.

10. Place a baking rack inside a baking pan with tall sides. Place the pork bag in the baking pan, cover it with foil all the way down to the pan, and bake for 1½ hours. Uncover, carefully turn with large forks (used to handle large pieces of meats), rub with more blood orange, re-cover, and bake 1½ hours more. Uncover and carefully turn over again with the large forks, rub with more blood orange, keep uncovered, increase the temperature to 475°F, and once it reaches 450°F, cook for 20 to 25 minutes more or until golden and crispy on top.

11. Remove the pork bag from the pan and set aside to rest for 15 minutes. Carve and serve with Sweet Plantain Wedges (page 129) or Baked Sweet Plantain Boats (page 130) and The Magic Is Strong! Spicy Ají (page 26) and Cilantro Pachanguero Salsa (page 28). For a sweet ending, try Magical Realism Pastries (page 46).

**NOTES:** Ask your butcher to prepare the pork skin for you.

Take into consideration that even though it will be filled in layers since it is a rectangle that has no wide sides, the center will be much thicker than the sides. The idea behind filling the bag in layers is that you cut it from the top and find a serving with all the foods inside for every guest.

If you find yourself with extra pork and rice mixture that cannot fit into the crispy pork skin, a delicious option is to bake it in plantain leaves. Preheat the oven to 300°F. Cover an 8-by-10-inch and 2-inch-tall baking pan with roasted plantain leaves. Add the remaining filling and cover with more plantain leaves, ensuring it is well covered. Bake covered with foil for 1 hour, remove the foil, and continue baking for an additional 1 to 2 hours until the filling is thoroughly cooked. This results in a large tamale-like dish that can be served as a delightful side dish on the same day.

Chapter

**5**

# Seafood

**Difficulty:** Medium
**Prep time:** 1 hour to overnight | **Cook time:** 0 minutes
**Yield:** 4 to 6 servings
**GF, DF**

# La Costa's Finest Cocktail
## *Cóctel mixto*

Summer days in the coastal towns of Colombia, adorned with weather similar to Pepa's happiest moods, are the perfect scenario to enjoy this finest seafood cocktail recipe made with squid rings and shrimp.

Traditionally served in cups and sold in street carts called *casetas,* these seafood cocktails have become widely popular all over the territory. They are a delightful experience to relish while engaging in conversation and enjoying tropical tunes, such as the iconic song that Agustín skillfully performs on the piano in *Encanto.*

**For the seafood:**

¾ pound sliced raw squid rings

¾ pound deveined extra small shrimp (U40-U60)

**For the cocktail sauce:**

¼ cup lime juice

¼ cup minced red onion

¼ cup minced cilantro

¼ cup ketchup

2 teaspoons minced parsley

1 teaspoon Worcestershire sauce

½ teaspoon garlic paste

½ teaspoon salt

¼ teaspoon freshly-ground black pepper

¼ teaspoon Tabasco sauce

¼ cup olive oil

**NOTE:** Our take on the traditional squid and shrimp for these cocktail cups is straightforward: both are cooked for less than one minute to keep them tender, then quickly chilled, and finally immersed into the delectable cocktail sauce.

1. To prepare the seafood: In a large pot over medium heat, bring 4 cups water to a boil. Add the squid and shrimp, cook for 50 seconds, drain, and chill in a bowl of iced water.

2. To make the cocktail sauce: In a medium bowl, mix the lime juice, onion, cilantro, ketchup, parsley, Worcestershire sauce, garlic paste, salt, freshly-ground black pepper, and Tabasco, and set aside for 10 minutes or more. Add the olive oil and mix well. Add the squid and shrimp to the bowl with the sauce, mix, and serve with Double Magic Plantain Discs (see page 126) or saltine crackers.

**Difficulty:** Medium
**Prep time:** 30 minutes | **Cook time:** 50 minutes
**Yield:** 8 appetizer servings
**GF, DF**

# Latin-Style Dancing Octopus Ceviche
## *Ceviche de pulpo*

Widely enjoyed in Colombia's islands and coastal towns, this flavorful ceviche recipe is perfect for any *Encanto*-inspired celebration.

Experience a burst of flavor with every bite of our tender octopus dish, enhanced by the fresh ingredients we use, such as red onion, tomato, lime juice, garlic, and cilantro. This delicious savory gift will keep you dancing all night long!

### For the octopus

2 pounds raw octopus tentacles (about 2½ cups, cooked & diced)

½ onion, quartered

6 cloves, whole

4 cumin seeds, cracked

3 bay leaves, crumbled

1 teaspoon anise seeds, cracked

1 clove garlic, minced

¼ teaspoon freshly-ground black pepper

### For the sauce

½ cup diced red onion (about ½ onion)

½ cup seeded and diced tomato (about 1 tomato)

2 tablespoons lime juice

1 clove garlic, minced

1 teaspoon salt

½ teaspoon freshly-ground black pepper

½ teaspoon habanero pepper (optional)

3 tablespoons minced cilantro

5 tablespoons olive oil

1. To make the octopus: In the pot of a pressure cooker, place the octopus, cover with water, and add the onion quarters, cloves, cumin, bay leaves, anise seeds, garlic, and freshly-ground black pepper, cover, and cook at high pressure for 45 minutes. Remove the cooked octopus tentacles from the stock, place them on a cutting board, and set aside to cool, about 10 minutes. Slice into ½-inch pieces.

2. To make the sauce: In a medium bowl, mix the onion, tomato, lime juice, garlic, salt, freshly-ground black pepper, and habanero pepper, if using. Add the cilantro and oil when ready to serve.

3. Add the pieces of octopus to the sauce, mix, and refrigerate to serve cold, about 1 hour, and keep refrigerated.

4. Dancing Octopus Ceviche is usually served in small cups or servings as an appetizer, and can also be served with Double Magic Plantain Discs (page 126) or Golden Cassava Fries (page 123).

**Difficulty:** Easy
**Prep time:** 45 minutes | **Cook time:** 1½ hours
**Yield:** 6 large servings
**GF, DF**

# Clay-Baked Coconut Fish
## *Viudo de pescado*

Traditionally in Colombia, coconut-flavored fish is baked in clay pots layered with plantain or palm leaves, which grow in regions like the one seen in *Encanto*.

Our version of this recipe replaces the clay pots with regular ones while still incorporating the leaves. Although brittle, plantain (or *bijao*) leaves are softened by passing them over a fire and imparting a deep green shine. This prepares them to serve as vessels for the vegetables and fish.

Clay-Baked Coconut Fish is a perfect dish for cold evenings outdoors. We picture *la familia* Madrigal under the stars, wrapped in ruanas, watching the fish bake slowly in a clay pot over the fire.

2 cups (about 2 recipes' worth) Familia's Sofrito (page 17)

2 plantain leaves, fresh or frozen

3 tablespoons olive oil

1 small green plantain, peeled, halved, and cut into 1½-inch chunks

1 pound cassava, peeled and quartered lengthwise

½ pound cheeky yam, peeled and sliced lengthwise into ½-inch strips

½ pound winter squash, peeled and cut into 1-inch pieces

½ pound yam, peeled and cut into 1-inch dice

Six 6-ounce fillets or steaks of pike fish or other white fish

2 teaspoons salt

½ teaspoon freshly-ground black pepper

12 sprigs cilantro

2 cups coconut milk

2 cups fish stock (or 2 teaspoons seafood bouillon base concentrate and 2 cups of water)

1 small ripe unpeeled plantain, cut into 1½-inch pieces

4 cups Candlelight White Rice (page 107)

1. Prepare the Familia's Sofrito.
2. If using the fresh plantain leaves, slowly pass them over the stove's flame, on both sides. If no gas stove is available, you can use a kitchen torch. Remove the center vein and place in a large pot crosswise to cover the bottom. The leaves should be long enough to cover the pot at the end of the recipe. Spread the oil on the leaves. If using the frozen plantain leaves, defrost and then unroll them. They are then ready to use.
3. Add the green plantains, cassava, and cheeky yam into the leaf covered pot. Over them, place the squash and yam. Spread half of the Familia's Sofrito over the vegetables. Place the fish steaks over the vegetables, sprinkle with the salt, freshly-ground black pepper, add 6 sprigs of the cilantro, and pour the coconut milk and stock into the pot. Cover with the plantain leaves hanging on the sides, if using, or with the pot lid. Over medium-high heat, bring the mixture to a boil, then reduce heat to low and simmer for 50 minutes.
4. Prepare the Candlelight White Rice (page 107).
5. In a small pot over medium-high heat, place 4 cups water and add the ripe plantain pieces. Bring to a boil, reduce the temperature to medium-low, and simmer for 15 minutes. Remove from the heat and set aside to keep warm.
6. Open the pot with the fish and vegetables and open the leaves on top and let them hang over the side of the pot. Remove the fish from the pot, and transfer each steak to a plate. Serve with a chunk of sweet plantain, and some of the vegetables from the pot. Pour the coconut milk onto each plate, then serve with Candlelight White Rice (page 107), and a dollop of the remaining Familia's Sofrito. Decorate with the remaining sprigs of cilantro.

**NOTE:** Peel the boiled sweet plantains before you eat them, as the skin is not edible.

**Difficulty:** Medium
**Prep time:** 25 minutes | **Cook time:** 2 minutes
**Yield:** 6 servings
**GF, DF**

# Zesty and Exceptional Fish Ceviche
## Ceviche de pescado

Lime juice works its citrusy magic on fish in this recipe, transforming it from raw to cooked and enhancing its delicious taste.

This ability to shape-shift, like Camilo, adds a zesty flavor to these ocean and river treasures, all without requiring fire or heat. Just pure and refreshing wonder!

Note that this recipe takes two days to prepare.

1¼ pounds corvina or any fresh white fish, cut into ½-inch cubes (or ⅛-inch slices)

2 cups lime juice (about 16 limes)

¾ cup diced red onion (about 1 medium onion)

½ cup peeled, seeded, and diced tomato (about 1 tomato)

¼ cup minced cilantro

2 teaspoons salt

1½ teaspoons freshly-ground black pepper

½ teaspoon minced habanero pepper (optional)

6 tablespoons olive oil

Saltine crackers, for serving

**DAY 1**

1.  In a medium bowl, mix the fish cubes with the lime juice. Refrigerate until the fish turns white, 3 to 5 hours or overnight.

**DAY 2**

2.  In a large bowl, place the fish, and add the onion, tomato, cilantro, salt, freshly-ground black pepper, and habanero, if using. Marinate for 30 minutes, drain through a sieve, and discard the liquid. Flavors mature and soften after sitting together for some time. Place the drained mixture back into the bowl and add the olive oil. Serve immediately or refrigerate until ready to serve. Saltine crackers are still served with ceviche all over the country, as well as Double Magic Plantain Discs (page 126), Golden Cassava Fries (page 123), and yam chips.

**NOTE:** You can make this recipe and serve it with raw fish that is thinly sliced instead of diced but reduce the amount of lime juice to ¼ cup. For the sliced raw-style ceviche, cut the onion and tomatoes into thin slices too and do not drain.

**Difficulty:** Easy
**Prep time:** 15 minutes | **Cook time:** 5 minutes
**Yield:** 2 to 4 servings
**GF**

# Glowing Garlic Butter Crab Claws
## *Muelas de cangrejo*

Having access to both the Pacific Coast and the Caribbean, Colombia's seafood recipe list is anything but short! Crab soup could surely boost Pepa Madrigal's mood, while Agustín could enjoy sharing a platter of crab claws with his three daughters.

With so many options, we invite you to join the crab claw frenzy with this easy-to-make and easy-to-love recipe featuring butter, garlic, and a touch of lime. Though a bit messy, dipping the cool claws in this glowing buttery gift is worth it, and would be a hit with the Madrigal grandkids.

½ teaspoon bouillon base concentrate (see note)

6 tablespoons butter

2 tablespoons garlic paste

2 tablespoons minced parsley, plus extra for serving

2 pounds precooked crab claws, thawed, if frozen, and rinsed

1 lemon, cut into wedges

**NOTE:** A ½ cup of fish or shrimp stock with ½ cup water can be used instead of the bouillon base concentrate and water.

1. Mix 1 cup water with the bouillon base concentrate.

2. In a large sauté pan over medium heat, place the butter and garlic paste, and sauté until the butter has dissolved and the garlic is aromatic, about 30 seconds. Add the bouillon mixture, parsley, and crab claws and cook until most of the water has evaporated, 3 to 5 minutes.

3. Serve on a platter, sprinkle with more parsley, and serve with the lemon wedges.

**Difficulty:** Medium
**Prep time:** 10 minutes
**Cook time:** 8 to 12 minutes
**Yield:** 4 to 6 servings | **GF\*, DF**

# Encanto River Crispy Fried Fish
## *Pescado frito*

People in Colombia often rejoice by gathering near glistening beaches and mystical riverbeds, like the one Mirabel sits beside to reflect on and then connect with her abuela on a deeper emotional level.

The Encanto River Crispy Fried Fish recipe uses a simple yet flavorful salt and lime marinade to infuse the fish with tanginess and joy when deep-fried.

Four 4-to-6-pound whole yellowtails or red snappers, or 4 individual silverbelly fish (mojarra), scaled and gutted

½ teaspoon salt

1 teaspoon lime juice

1 cup wheat or corn flour

4 to 6 cups sunflower oil, for frying

2 limes, cut into wedges

1 teaspoon minced parsley

**Specialty Tools:**
Kitchen thermometer

1. Make 3 or 4 slits along both sides of the fish and rub it with the salt and lime juice. Coat it in the flour, shaking off any excess.

2. Line a plate with paper towels. Place the oil in a large pot and bring to 350°F. Deep-fry the fish for 6 to 8 minutes, turn, and fry for an additional 4 to 6 minutes until golden and crispy. Remove from the oil, place on the prepared plate to drain excess oil, and serve with the lime wedges and a sprinkle of the minced parsley.

3. Serve with Double Magic Plantain Discs (see page 126), Dazzling White Coconut Rice (page 106) or Freckled Coconut Rice (page 108), and Open Door House Salad (page 32).

**NOTES:** Use a rounded and high-sided pot that is just about as wide as your fish so you can turn it without wasting too much oil.

This recipe is gluten free if using corn flour.

# Fried Fish Steaks from the Rainbow River
## Posta de pescado

*Encanto* is inspired by Colombia's natural marvels, like the striking colors of the river where Alma finds Mirabel, and they embrace, surrounded by yellow butterflies.

Different regions in our country have unique ways of cooking a wide variety of fish from our tropical rivers and oceans. One popular method is to fillet or cut the fish into horseshoe-style pieces or steaks, then lightly dust them with flour and season them with simple ingredients for a delicious pan-fried Colombian delicacy.

¼ cup minced scallion, green and white parts (about 1 scallion)

1½ tablespoons lime juice

½ teaspoon salt

Four ¼-pound white mackerel fish steaks (any long, slim white fish will do)

¼ cup corn or wheat flour

½ cup sunflower oil, for frying

¼ cup chopped parsley

2 limes, cut into wedges, for serving

**Specialty Tools:**
Kitchen thermometer

**NOTES:** Consider serving with any of the sauces from chapter one, be it a raw sauce on the side or a cooked sauce over the hot fish.

This recipe is gluten free if using corn flour.

1. In a ramekin, mix the scallions, lime juice, and salt, and rub the mixture over the fish steaks. Let them sit for 2 minutes, then lightly dust in the flour, shaking off any excess.

2. Line a plate with paper towels. In a large sauté pan over medium heat, add the oil and bring to 350°F. Add the fish steaks, one at a time, and pan fry for 4 minutes per side, remove from the pan, and place on the prepared plate to drain excess oil. Sprinkle the fish steaks with the parsley and serve with the lime wedges and Open Door House Salad (page 32), Dazzling White Coconut Rice (page 106), and Double Magic Plantain Discs (page 126).

Chapter

**6**

# Rice

**Difficulty:** Easy
**Prep time:** 25 minutes | **Cook time:** 35 minutes
**Yield:** 8 to 10 servings
**GF, DF**

# Caribbean Starlight Seafood Rice
## *Arroz con mariscos*

Enjoy this Caribbean Starlight Seafood Rice with loved ones. As the fishermen set out to sea, the night sky reveals the bounty of fish under its star-studded constellations.

Every day, fishermen catch the ocean and rivers' treasures and transport them across rugged mountains on trusty donkeys like the ones Luisa carries. The food is then prepared at home when they return to their families. It is a wonderful chain of love and miracles!

6 tablespoons olive oil

2 tablespoons garlic paste

1 tablespoon achiote paste or ½ tablespoon turmeric

1 teaspoon curry powder

2 teaspoons salt

1 teaspoon freshly-ground black pepper

1 cup diced scallions, green and white parts (about 4 scallions)

½ cup grated yellow onion (about ½ onion)

½ cup grated red bell pepper (about ½ pepper)

¼ cup minced sweet peppers (about 4 sweet peppers)

2-pound bag of frozen seafood mix (shrimp, calamari, octopus, clams)

5 cups hot water

2½ cups white rice

2 teaspoons fish bouillon base concentrate

3 tablespoons chopped parsley

1. In a large pot over medium heat, place the oil, garlic paste, achiote paste, curry powder, salt, and freshly-ground black pepper and mix for 1 minute. Add the scallions, onion, bell pepper, and sweet peppers, and sauté for 8 minutes more. Add the seafood, mix and sauté for 5 minutes. Add the hot water, rice, and bouillon base concentrate and bring to a boil. Reduce the heat to low, cover, and cook for 20 minutes.

2. Fluff the rice, sprinkle with the parsley, and serve with Sweet Plantain Wedges (page 129) or Baked Sweet Plantain Boats (page 130) and Uno, Dos, Tres Avocado Spread (page 31).

**Difficulty:** Difficult
**Prep time:** 35 minutes | **Cook time:** 2 hours
**Yield:** 8 to 12 servings
**GF, DF**

# "Make Your Family Proud" Sticky Rice
## *Arroz atollado*

Is it soup or is it rice? Mysteriously, it's both! *Arroz atollado* is a fusion of soup and rice from Colombia's Valle del Cauca. It features aromatic cumin-scented pork, chicken, or beef in a warm and saucy dish.

Julieta might call it a miracle! Just one spoonful of this sticky rice is so comforting it could make anyone feel better.

### For the stock:
1 tablespoon olive oil

6 pork soup bones

1 pound pork or beef, cut in ½-inch dice

½ cup diced yellow onion (about 1 onion)

½ cup diced tomato (about ½ tomato)

3 cloves garlic

3 bay leaves

¼ teaspoon freshly-ground black pepper

6 chicken breasts, with bone

### For the seasoning:
4 chorizos, sliced ½-inch thick

5 tablespoons olive oil (if needed)

3 cups minced scallions, white and green parts (about 12 scallions)

3 cups peeled, seeded, and finely diced tomatoes (about 10 tomatoes)

3 tablespoons garlic paste

2 teaspoons sugar

3 teaspoons beef bouillon base concentrate

2 teaspoons salt

2 teaspoons ground cumin

2 teaspoons achiote paste or 1 teaspoon turmeric

1 cup minced cilantro (about 1 bunch)

### For the rice:
2 cups white rice

2 teaspoons salt

### For serving:
½ cup minced cilantro

2 to 4 sliced Fuerte (or other large) avocados (or 4 to 6 Hass)

**NOTE:** To remove the fat from the saucy rice, follow these steps. With a spoon, remove the visible fat that floats on the top or settles on the side of the pot. Some of the soupy rice will come with the fat. Place it on a flat baking pan and freeze for 5 minutes. The sauce will not freeze, but the fat will set, so you can easily remove it with a small spoon. Place the rice back into the pot, it will be warm by mixing it with the rest of the rice.

You can also use paper towels. Pass over the sides of the cooking pot to absorb the fat. Discard the paper towels.

1. To make the stock: In a large pressure cooker, add 1 tablespoon of the olive oil, the pork soup bones, and pork or beef, and sauté until lightly browned, 4 to 5 minutes. Add 8 cups water, the onion, tomato, garlic, bay leaves, and freshly-ground black pepper. Cover and cook under pressure for 35 minutes (if using a regular pot on a stovetop, cook for 1½ hours, covered). Add the chicken and pressure cook for 8 minutes more (on a regular stovetop, cook for 20 minutes, covered). Remove the meats, strain the stock retaining the stock liquid in two 4-cup measuring cups, and set aside. Remove the fat (see page 104). You should have 8 cups cooking liquid. (Add stock or water if missing some.)

2. To make the seasoning: In a large pot over medium-low heat, cook the chorizos for 5 minutes to render some of their fat, leaving 4 tablespoons of fat in the pan. If not enough, add the olive oil to complete. Add the scallions, tomatoes, garlic paste, sugar, bouillon base concentrate, salt, cumin, and achiote paste, mix, and cook, covered, for 15 to 20 minutes, until it becomes a chunky sauce. Add the cilantro and save half the sauce in the pot and pour the other half of the sauce in a separate large pot.

3. To make the rice: In the separate large pot with the sauce over medium-high heat, add the rice and salt and mix for 1 minute. Add the pork or beef and 8 cups of stock and simmer for 30 minutes.

4. To serve: The rice will have a saucy consistency. Sprinkle with the cilantro and serve with a piece of avocado and either Sweet Plantain Wedges (page 129) or Baked Sweet Plantain Boats (page 130), and Charming Sauce (page 19).

**Difficulty:** Easy
**Prep time:** 5 minutes (plus 20 minutes, if making the coconut milk)
**Cook time:** 20 minutes
**Yield:** 8 servings | **GF, DF, V**

# Dazzling White Coconut Rice
## *Arroz blanco con coco*

When life gives you coconuts, indulge in the magic of this Dazzling White Coconut Rice!

Children like the Madrigals would surely compete to find the softest dent on each coconut and crack it open to release its sweet, silky water. It's a gift from nature!

2 cups rice

2 teaspoons sugar

2 teaspoons salt

4 cups coconut milk (freshly made from 2 to 3 coconuts [see page 23] or mixed canned coconut milks [see note])

**NOTE:** Canned coconut milk is higher in fat than the fresh variety. If using canned, mix it with half of boxed coconut milk (to drink) or water, then use.

1. In a medium pot over medium heat, place the rice, sugar, salt, and coconut milk and mix until the sugar has dissolved, about 1 minute. Bring to a boil. After about 7 minutes, or as soon as you see the rice on the surface, cover the pot and reduce the heat to low. Cook covered for 20 minutes.

2. Uncover, fluff the rice, and serve.

3. Dazzling White Coconut Rice is traditionally served like Candlelight White Rice (page 107), gently pressed into a cup and plated without the customary dent. This exquisite creation is usually a side dish for many traditional coastal dishes.

# Candlelight White Rice
## *Arroz blanco*

No supper with the *familia* Madrigal is ready until the white rice is cooked.

A staple side dish in many Colombian homes, *arroz blanco* is a fundamental part of everyday meals but also great to accompany fancy dishes as it complements the enchanting flavors of a variety of soups and stews.

Use a cup or a small bowl to shape it into a mountain or turn it into a magical volcano by adding a spoonful of Charming Sauce (page 19) on top.

1 cup white rice

½ teaspoon salt

½ teaspoon olive oil

**NOTE:** The white rice takes the same time to cook when sautéed or boiled. These are just different methods of starting off the white rice.

1. Stovetop boiling method: Place the rice, salt, olive oil, and 2 cups water in a small pot over medium-high heat. Once it comes to a boil, allow most of the water to evaporate until small, round, crater-like holes appear on the surface of the rice, about 5 minutes into the cooking time. Immediately set the heat to low, cover the pot, and cook covered for 15 minutes. Do not uncover the pot as it will let out all the steam and cook unevenly. Uncover, fluff the rice, and serve.

2. Stovetop sauté method: Place the rice, salt, and olive oil in a small pot over medium-high heat to sauté.

3. Stir constantly for 1 to 2 minutes, until the rice is lightly toasted and fragrant. Add 2 cups water to the pot and stir to combine. Once it comes to a boil, allow most of the water to evaporate until small, round, crater-like holes appear on the surface of the rice, about 5 minutes into the cooking time. Immediately set the heat to low, cover the pot, and cook covered for 15 minutes. Do not uncover the pot as it will let out all the steam and cook unevenly. Uncover, fluff the rice, and serve.

4. Instant pot or pressure cooker method: Place the rice, salt, olive oil, and 1¼ cups water in the pressure cooker's bowl. Cook with pressure for 8 minutes. Let the steam out and serve.

5. To serve, press rice into round-bottomed coffee cups, turn onto side or salad plates, then press a dent on the top of the rice, to resemble a mountain with a crater.

**Difficulty:** Medium
**Prep time:** 5 minutes (plus 20 minutes, if making the coconut milk)
**Cook time:** 50 minutes
**Yield:** 8 servings | **GF, DF, V**

# Freckled Coconut Rice
## *Arroz con coco titoté*

Beware! This recipe yields unexpected and magical results! The secret to Freckled Coconut Rice is *titoté*. As the coconut milk simmers, it transforms into enchanting dark brown freckles and rich coconut oil that grace the pan's bottom. The *titoté* intensifies the coconut flavor, infusing every grain of rice, and the raisins plump up when added.

This dish is beloved by both kids and adults for its fancy-looking freckles and tropical aroma. It's often served at family gatherings and special occasions, similar to the magical gift ceremonies at the housewarming parties with the Madrigals after the rebuilding of Casita.

4 cups coconut milk (freshly made [page XX] or mixed canned coconut milk [see note])

2 cups rice

¼ cup raisins

1½ tablespoons brown sugar

2 teaspoons salt

**NOTE:** Canned coconut milk is higher in fat than the fresh variety. This is why we mix it with half of the boxed coconut milk (to drink) or water, then use it, and why it takes longer to become the *titoté*, thus requires more cooking time.

1. In a medium pot or caldero over medium-high heat, place the coconut milk and heat for 20 minutes (up to 40 minutes with canned milk mix, see note), until the milk becomes an oil with brownish crumbs at the bottom of the pot. Scrape the pot to release all the crumbs. It is ready when the white milk has been replaced with crumbs and coconut oil. Leave 2 tablespoons of the coconut oil only in the pot and discard the rest.

2. Add the rice, raisins, brown sugar, and salt, and mix well. The raisins will plump in the oil. Add 4 cups water, bring to a boil, and cook until you see the rice near the surface, about 3 minutes. Cover, reduce the heat to low, and cook for 20 minutes.

3. Uncover, fluff the rice, and serve.

**Difficulty:** Easy
**Prep Time:** 5 minutes (plus 20 minutes, if making the coconut milk)
**Cook time:** 30 minutes
**Yield:** 8 to 10 servings | **GF, DF, V, V+**

# Black-Eyed Peas Sticky Rice
## *Arroz de frijol de cabecita negra*

This whimsical sticky dish is made with your choice of coconut milk or vegetable stock. The rice is cooked together with the protein-packed flavors of the black-eyed peas, resulting in a delightful cloud of goodness, so comforting and satisfying that it could be served as a standalone meal or a side dish, boundless enough to feed the whole Madrigal family and their beloved neighbors and friends.

½ pound dry black-eyed peas

1 tablespoon olive oil

1 yellow onion, diced

2 cloves garlic, mashed

2 teaspoons salt

½ teaspoon curry powder

¼ teaspoon freshly-ground black pepper

2 cups coconut milk (freshly made [see page 23] or canned mixed with milk [see page 106])

2 cups white rice

1 cup vegetable stock

1. Place the dry black-eyed peas in a large bowl with 6 cups water. Set aside for 6 hours or overnight. Drain.

2. In the bowl of a pressure cooker, add the olive oil, onion, garlic, salt, curry, freshly-ground black pepper, coconut milk (or coconut milk mixture) and mix. Add the rice, rehydrated black-eyed peas, and stock, and mix. Pressure cook for 25 minutes.

3. Fluff the rice and serve with Sweet Plantain Wedges (page 129), Gift Ceremony Tomato Salsa (page 29), Open Door House Salad (page 32), or Uno, Dos, Tres Avocado Spread (page 31). Sometimes in Colombia it is also served with Magic Doorknob Meat Powder (page 74).

**Difficulty:** Medium
**Prep time:** 30 minutes | **Cook time:** 30 minutes
**Yield:** 8 to 10 servings
**GF, DF**

# Special Gift Chicken and Rice
## *Arroz con pollo*

A special gift for your taste buds! This recipe features a colorful medley of vegetables, including carrots, green beans, peas, bell peppers, and onions, combined with Colombian rice infused with achiote for a delicious and unique flavor.

Bursting with vibrant colors, much like the flowers of Isabela that bloom as she embraces her true self, this dish is the magical door to healthy eating and a newfound love for veggies in both grown-ups and kids.

### For the chicken and stock:

4 whole bone-in chicken breasts, skin removed

1 pound chicken wings

2 medium yellow onions, chopped

2 carrots, quartered

1 red bell pepper, chopped

10 sprigs cilantro

2 cloves garlic, mashed

1 teaspoon chicken bouillon base concentrate

1 teaspoon salt

¼ teaspoon freshly-ground black pepper

### For the vegetables and rice:

3 tablespoons olive oil

1 teaspoon achiote paste or ½ teaspoon turmeric

2 teaspoons minced garlic

1 teaspoon cumin

2 teaspoons salt

¼ teaspoon freshly-ground black pepper

1 cup diced scallions, white and green parts (about 4 scallions)

1 cup diced carrots (about 2 carrots)

1 red bell pepper, diced

1 cup fresh peas

3 tablespoons tomato paste

2 tablespoons Worcestershire sauce

2 tablespoons coconut aminos

2 cups white rice

### For serving:

¼ cup minced parsley

¼ cup minced cilantro

4 avocados, quartered

1. To make the chicken and stock: In a medium pot over medium-high heat, place the chicken breasts and wings, 6 cups water, the onions, carrots, red bell pepper, cilantro, garlic, bouillon base concentrate, salt, and freshly-ground black pepper. Bring to a boil, cover the pot, reduce the heat to medium-low, and simmer for 15 minutes. Remove the chicken breasts from the pot and set aside on a plate to shred. Measure the cooking liquid in the pot and reserve 8 cups for the rice preparation.

2. To make the vegetables and rice: In a large pot over medium heat, place the oil, achiote paste, garlic, cumin, salt, and freshly-ground black pepper and mix for 1 minute. Add the scallions, carrots, bell pepper, peas, tomato paste, Worcestershire sauce, and coconut aminos, mix, and cook for 5 minutes more. Add the rice and the reserved 8 cups of prepared stock from the pot, increase the heat to medium-high and bring to a boil. When the rice makes eyes (round, crater-like rings on the surface of the rice), reduce the heat to low, cover, and cook for 15 minutes.

3. Shred the chicken breasts and set the wings aside to use in another recipe. Add the shredded chicken to the cooked rice, mix to fluff, sprinkle the parsley and cilantro and serve with the sliced avocados, Baked Sweet Plantain Boats (page 130), Gift Ceremony Tomato Salsa (page 29), and Open Door House Salad (page 32).

Chapter

**7**

# Side Dishes

**Difficulty:** Easy
**Prep time:** 15 minutes
**Cook time:** 30 minutes
**Yield:** 8 servings | **GF, V**

# Spilled Creamy Potatoes
## *Papas chorreadas*

From the beautiful Colombian Andes, *Papas chorreadas* is a classic dish that literally translates to "spilled potatoes."

These creamy potatoes are a secret worth sharing, much like when Dolores revealed the shocking news that Mirabel broke into Bruno's tower to find her uncle's last vision.

1½ pounds small red potatoes (about 8 potatoes)

1½ tablespoons salt

2½ tablespoons oil

2 cups scallions cut into 3-inch long pieces (about 10 scallions)

2 cloves garlic, mashed

1 cup peeled, seeded, and diced tomatoes (about 3 tomatoes)

¼ teaspoon cumin

¼ teaspoon freshly-ground black pepper

1½ cups vegetable stock

¾ cup milk

¾ cup heavy cream or half-and-half

6 ounces of grated white farmer cheese or shredded mozzarella

1. Wash the potatoes well and peel them unevenly, leaving about half of the skin on.

2. In a medium pot over medium-low heat, place the potatoes, 1 tablespoon of the salt, and water to cover the potatoes, cover with a lid, and cook for 15 to 20 minutes or until tender. Pass through a sieve and set aside.

3. In a large sauté pan, heat the oil over medium-low heat, add the scallions and garlic and sauté for 2 to 3 minutes until aromatic. Add the tomatoes, cumin, the remaining ½ tablespoon salt, and freshly-ground black pepper, stir, and cook 7 minutes more to a saucy consistency. Add the stock, milk, and cream, mix well, and cook covered for 5 minutes or until slightly thickened. Add the cheese and stir until the cheese has melted.

4. Pour over the cooked potatoes and serve as a side dish alongside beef dishes like Magic Doorknob Meat Powder (page 74), Townspeople Creole Steak (page 79), Beef Fillet with Golden Onions (page 77), or Amazing Shredded Beef (page 76).

**Difficulty:** Easy
**Prep time:** 15 minutes (plus 30 minutes to rehydrate the dry lentils)
**Cook time:** 15 minutes
**Yield:** 8 to 10 servings | **GF, DF, V**

# Colombian Power Lentils
## *Lentejas*

In just minutes, these small brown legumes can be transformed into soup, patties, or full meals as versatile as Casita itself.

*Lentejas* are a great source of iron and energy, helping to build strong bones and muscles, making one as strong as Luisa. This recipe only requires one pot and is based on the traditional two-pot recipe, which typically yields a thick and saucy dish.

1 pound dry lentils (about 2 cups)

2 tablespoons olive oil

1 teaspoon achiote paste or ½ teaspoon turmeric

4 whole scallions, minced

3 cloves garlic, minced

¼ teaspoon cumin

2 carrots, halved

2 tomatoes, halved

2 yellow onions, halved

1 red bell pepper, halved

2 ajíes dulces, seeded (sweet peppers)

¼ cup cilantro

1½ teaspoons salt

1 cup plain Greek yogurt

1. Place the lentils in a medium bowl and cover them with water. Set aside for 30 minutes or more. This will rehydrate the lentils before cooking.

2. In the pot of a pressure cooker, place the oil, achiote paste, scallions, garlic, and cumin, and sauté for 1 minute or until fragrant. Add the carrots, lentils, and 4 cups water, and mix. If you have a basket or a pressure cooker top rack, place the tomatoes, onions, bell pepper, ajíes dulces, and cilantro on it, otherwise, just place them over the lentils, cover, and pressure cook for 15 minutes. Open, scoop out the garlic, onions, tomatoes, bell pepper, cilantro, and carrots, and transfer to a blender with 1 cup of cooking liquid and 1 cup lentils. Blend and transfer back to the pot, mix, add the salt, and serve.

3. Serve with a dollop of the Greek yogurt, Familia's Sofrito (page 17), Candlelight White Rice (page 107), Double Magic Plantain Discs (page 126), or Magic Doorknob Meat Powder (page 74).

**NOTE:** When a pressure cooker is unavailable, these can be cooked on the stovetop, in the same way, simply extending the 15-minute cooking time from the pressure cooker to 45 minutes.

**Difficulty:** Easy
**Prep time:** 15 minutes
**Cook time:** 30 to 45 minutes
**Yield:** 6 to 8 servings | **GF, DF, V+**

# New Foundation Salty Potatoes
## *Papa salada*

In the wondrous Encanto, where magic and teamwork are intertwined, these New Foundation Salty Potatoes could support Casita's stronger walls and floors.

Potatoes are essential in Colombian cuisine. Our Papa salada recipe uses russet potatoes to achieve crackling and crispy skins, and the right amount of salt to elevate their flavor.

3 pounds small russet potatoes, unpeeled and washed (about 12 potatoes)

1½ tablespoons salt

1. In a pot just large enough to be about 3 to 4 inches taller than the fitted potatoes, over medium heat, place the whole potatoes, salt, and enough water to barely cover them (about 1 inch above the potatoes). Cook covered for 30 to 45 minutes or until the water is almost completely evaporated. Take a small peek after 30 minutes. Turn off the heat, uncover the pot, and swirl the pot so the potatoes become salted.

2. Serve with Amazing Shredded Beef (page 76) or Beef Fillet with Golden Onions (page 77), or as a snack (when making the smaller sized ones) along with Firecracker Festival Beef and Pork Links (page 81).

**Difficulty:** Easy
**Prep time:** 5 minutes | **Cook time:** 30 minutes
**Yield:** 4 to 6 servings
**GF, V**

# Moonlight Baked Yellow Potatoes
## *Papita criolla asada*

Colombia's culinary landscape boasts a multitude of enchanting ingredients, including one of our favorites—the slightly sweet yellow potato variety.

After playing in his rainforest-inspired magical room, Antonio and his animal friends would surely enjoy this tasty snack. This recipe recreates traditional brick oven–cooked potatoes for all to savor.

2 tablespoons olive oil

1 teaspoon butter, softened

½ teaspoon salt

1 pound small yellow potatoes, unpeeled (about 8 potatoes)

1. Preheat the oven to 375°F.
2. In a medium bowl, add the oil, butter, and salt and mix. Add the potatoes and mix to cover them completely. Transfer to a baking dish.
3. Bake the potatoes for 30 to 35 minutes or until tender and lightly golden. Serve.
4. Moonlight Baked Yellow Potatoes are part of many dishes, such as Golden Chicken Stew (page 82) and Golden Pork and Beef Empanadas (page 48), due to their mild sweetness and delicate texture. They can be enjoyed on their own as delectable bites or served as a side dish alongside Famous Colombian Fried Pork Belly (page 85) or Firecracker Festival Beef and Pork Links (page 81).

**Difficulty:** Difficult
**Prep time:** 45 minutes | **Cook time:** 30 minutes
**Yield:** 8 to 10 servings
**GF**

# "What a Joyous Day" Cassava Fritters
## *Carimañolas de queso*

*Carimañolas* are delicious cassava fritters often served for breakfast or at celebrations, such as Felix and Pepa's wedding.

Their distinctive oval shape and pointed edges are formed by shaping cooked ground cassava. Filled with a variety of ingredients, including cheese, meat, poultry, and more, *carimañolas* are incredibly tasty and are sure to bring joy to your day!

2 pounds peeled yuca, fresh or frozen

3 teaspoons salt

A pinch of allspice powder
(less than ⅛ teaspoon)

¾ pound (2 cups) white farmer
cheese, grated

4 cups sunflower oil

**Specialty Tools:**
Kitchen thermometer

1. Cut the yuca in half lengthwise, remove the center stem, and cut crosswise into 3 pieces. In a medium pot, bring 2 quarts water and 2 teaspoons of the salt to a boil. Add the yuca and allspice and cook for 20 to 30 minutes. A fork should go through but still have a little resistance (not mushy). Drain and dry well with paper towels.

2. Sprinkle the yuca with ½ teaspoon of the salt and mash with a potato masher, or puree with a mixer at low speed to a stiff puree you can mold. Transfer to a large bowl. Divide into 12 pieces, place on parchment paper, and press each one into about a 4-inch wide ⅓-inch thick oval.

3. In a small bowl, add the cheese and the remaining ½ teaspoon salt, if not salted, and mix to a rough paste.

4. Place each piece of flattened yuca onto your palm, curl your hand, and add the cheese to the center, pressing it inside. Close your hand to cover the cheese and press to seal on all sides, shaping into an oval ball.

5. Line a plate with paper towels. In a large pot, place the oil and heat to 350°F. Deep-fry the fritters for 3 to 4 minutes until lightly golden on all sides. Remove and set on the prepared plate to drain.

6. Serve with Familia's Sofrito (page 17), Charming Sauce (page 19), The Magic Is Strong! Spicy Ají (page 26), or just as they are.

**Difficulty:** Medium
**Prep time:** 15 minutes | **Cook time:** 40 minutes
**Yield:** 6 to 8 servings
**GF, V\*, V+\***

# Did Someone Say Beans?
## *Frijoles*

With effortless grace, Isabela, the family's golden child, arrived on a vibrant vine in *Encanto* and asked, "Did someone say flowers?" Her magical gift instantly relieved the party planners' stress and left everyone awestruck.

If the menu features delicious, full-bodied, and saucy red beans, their sweet aroma will entice loved ones to the table in seconds. Surely the Madrigal children would eagerly rush down the stairs of Casita to enjoy them, and the entire family would be stress-free and awestruck with the taste of this dish.

Our version of this traditional recipe features fresh scallions, tomatoes, carrots, cilantro, and a blend of spices, creating a gluten and dairy-free meal that is nourishing and delicious.

And, like Isabela said, "Please, don't clap!"

1 pound dry red beans (about 2½ cups)

3 tablespoons olive oil

1½ cups sliced scallions, white and green parts (about 5 scallions)

1½ cups peeled and diced tomatoes (about 3 tomatoes)

¼ teaspoon ground cumin

¼ teaspoon freshly-ground black pepper

¼ cup minced cilantro

2 carrots

8 cilantro stems

¼ teaspoon salt

1 pound ham hock or oxtail (optional)

1. Place the beans in a medium bowl and cover them with 7 cups water. Set aside for 6 hours or more, then discard the water. This will rehydrate the beans before cooking.

2. In the pot of a pressure cooker, place the oil, scallions, tomatoes, cumin, freshly-ground black pepper, and cilantro. Sauté for 6 minutes. Add the rehydrated beans, carrots, cilantro, salt, 4 cups water (ensure it covers 1 inch above the beans, so add more if needed), and the ham hock or oxtail, if using. Cover and pressure cook for 35 minutes. Open, remove the bones, and scoop out 1 cup of cooking liquid and the cooked vegetables into a blender. Blend to a thick smooth sauce and transfer back to the pot. Adjust salt, mix, and serve.

**NOTES:** When a pressure cooker is unavailable, this dish can be cooked on the stovetop in the same way, simply extending the 35-minute cooking time from the pressure cooker to 1½ to 2 hours.

Did Someone Say Beans? are mostly made as a side to many meals in the region of Antioquia, also served with Charming Sauce (page 19), Magic Doorknob Meat Powder (page 74), Sweet Plantain Wedges (page 129), and are an essential part of Paisa Family Platter (page 73).

This recipe is vegetarian and vegan if prepared without the ham hock or oxtail.

**Difficulty:** Medium
**Prep time:** 20 minutes
**Cook time:** 20 minutes
**Yield:** 8 servings | **V**

# Cheesy Plantain Mochilas
## *Aborrajados*

Ripe sweet plantains and soft white cheese drenched in a flour sauce, then fried to crunchy goodness, *aborrajado* is a classic recipe from Valle del Cauca that surprises your palate with its taste.

Cheesy Plantain Mochilas are versatile and perfect for a family picnic by the river. Mirabel could easily bring them in her own *mochila!*

### For the plantains:

3 to 4 very ripe plantains

¾ pound white farmer cheese, cut into 8 rectangular pieces

2 to 3 cups sunflower oil, for frying

### For the batter:

1¼ cups all-purpose flour

½ teaspoon salt

½ teaspoon achiote paste or ¼ teaspoon turmeric

1 egg

1 to 2 tablespoons milk (if necessary, to thin the batter)

### Specialty Tools:

Kitchen thermometer

**NOTE:** In the more traditional method of cooking, the plantains are initially fried in a pot over medium heat at 350°F, for 3 to 4 minutes, rather than air frying (but, if your plantains have been refrigerated, lower the temperature to 350°F and cook for four minutes total).

1. To make the plantains: Cut the ends off each plantain and slice into 3 or 4 pieces. Cook in an air fryer at 380°F for 8 to 10 minutes, or until golden and soft in the middle. Set aside to cool. You can make them up to 6 hours in advance.

2. Line your work surface with a piece of parchment paper and place one piece of plantain on the paper. Push the plantain through one end, remove the peel, and flatten with your hands to about ⅓-inch thick. Repeat with the other plantain pieces.

3. With your hands wet, place the cheese in the center of the flattened plantain pieces. Place the parchment paper with the flattened plantain on the palm of your hand and wrap the plantain over the cheese. Seal the ends and sides together with the tips of your wet fingers and press to form an oval-shape fritter. Set aside on a plate until ready to fry.

4. To make the batter: In a large bowl, mix the flour, salt, achiote paste, egg, and ¾ cup water. If the batter is too thick, add the milk. Dip the cheese-filled plantains into the batter.

5. Line a plate with paper towels. In a medium pot over medium-high heat, add the oil. Once it reaches 375°F, add one or two plantain balls at a time so they do not stick to each other, and fry for about 45 seconds, or until lightly golden on all sides. Remove from the pot and drain on the prepared plate. Serve as a side or appetizer.

Difficulty: Easy
Prep time: 10 minutes | Cook time: 35 minutes
Yield: 6 to 8 servings
GF, DF, V+

# Golden Cassava Fries
## *Yuca frita*

Colombia's enchanting culinary heritage is captured in the flavors of cassava, which hold a special allure and mystique for traditional families like the Madrigals.

Yuca is versatile and fun. Its taste and shape can be transformed in as many ways as Camilo can shape-shift. Follow this recipe for crispy Golden Cassava Fries that would make a great side dish to any meal.

2 pounds yuca, fresh or frozen, peeled

2½ teaspoons salt

¼ cup olive oil or olive oil spray, if using an air fryer

4 cups sunflower oil, for frying

**Specialty Tools:**
Kitchen thermometer

**NOTES:** This recipe, developed from the original Colombian *Yuca guisada*, or *frita*, requires the cassava to be fully cooked, almost to the mushy stage, and then fried or baked.

Serve alongside Glowing Garlic Butter Crab Claws (page 97), Encanto River Crispy Fried Fish (page 98), or Fried Fish Steaks from the Rainbow River (page 99), or as an appetizer with The Magic Is Strong! Spicy Ají (page 26), Cilantro Pachanguero Salsa (page 28), Spice Lovers Peanut Ají (page 18), Uno, Dos, Tres Avocado Spread (page 31), or simply salted beef, roasted poultry, and grilled seafood.

1. Cut the yuca lengthwise in half, remove the center stem, and cut each half into 3 or 4 long pieces. In a large pot filled with plenty of water to cover them (4 to 5 cups) and 2 teaspoons of the salt, cook the yuca over high heat for 30 to 35 minutes. A fork should go through with no resistance (not mushy, but very soft). Drain and dry the yuca pieces over paper towels. Brush with olive oil, if using the air fryer.

2. To air fry: In an air fryer at 380°F, place the yuca sticks. Cook for 7 minutes, turn, and cook for 7 minutes more.

3. To fry: Line a plate with paper towels. In a medium pot over medium-high heat, bring the sunflower oil to 350°F. Add the yuca and deep-fry until golden and crispy outside, about 5 minutes. Remove to the prepared plate to drain, sprinkle with the remaining ½ teaspoon salt immediately so it sticks to the cassava, and serve.

**Difficulty:** Medium
**Prep time:** 20 minutes | **Cook time:** 40 minutes
**Yield:** 4 to 6 servings
**GF, V***

# Rainforest Cassava Stew
## Yuca guisada

Cassava grows best in low rainy lands like the wondrous environment in *Encanto*, where Pepa Madrigal's emotions can quickly change the weather.

Yuca, similar to potatoes, is a versatile ingredient widely used in homemade Colombian meals. It can be boiled, fried, or baked and used in soups or salads. This recipe uses a light butter sauce for a mood-boosting culinary experience.

**For the cassava:**

2 pounds peeled cassava (yuca), fresh or frozen

2 teaspoons salt

**For the light butter sauce:**

6 tablespoons butter

2 tablespoons garlic paste

1 ½ cups vegetable or chicken stock (or 1 ½ teaspoons vegetable or chicken bouillon base concentrate and 1 ½ cups water), divided

1 cup (about 1 recipe) To the Rhythm of the Creole Sauce (page 22)

1 cup Familia's Sofrito (page 17)

10 ounces white farmer cheese, grated

1. Preheat the oven to 375°F or air fryer to 380°F.

2. To make the cassava: Cut the fresh cassava lengthwise in half, remove the center stem, and cut each half into 3 or 4 long pieces. In a large pot over high heat, cook the cassava with plenty of water to cover it (about 6 cups) and 2 teaspoons of the salt for 35 to 40 minutes. A fork should go through with no resistance (almost mushy). Drain and transfer to a baking dish.

3. To make the light butter sauce: In a small sauté pan over medium heat, place the butter and garlic paste and sauté 30 seconds. Add the stock, heat for 1 more minute, and pour over the cooked cassava.

4. Prepare To the Rhythm of the Creole Sauce (page 22), and when done, add the vegetable stock, mix, and set aside.

5. Pour Familia's Sofrito over the buttered cassava. Pour the To the Rhythm of the Creole Sauce over the Familia's Sofrito. Sprinkle the cassava with the cheese, and bake for 8 minutes or air fry for 5 minutes, or until the cheese melts. Serve.

**NOTE:** This recipe is vegetarian if prepared with vegetable stock or bouillon base concentrate.

**Difficulty:** Medium
**Prep time:** 25 minutes | **Cook time:** 15 minutes
**Yield:** 6 to 8 servings (10 patacones)
**GF, DF, V, V+**

# Double Magic Plantain Discs
## *Patacones*

A tasty and fun-to-make treat that would certainly keep los primos Madrigal busy helping in the kitchen, patacones are green plantains sliced into chunks, which are then fried, smashed into thin discs, and fried again until golden and crispy.

These Double Magic Plantain Discs are the perfect addition to any meal! Whether you're looking for a tasty side dish or a delicious appetizer, they can be served with a variety of dipping sauces or simply sprinkled with salt. They're sure to be a delectable gift for everyone in the family!

2 green plantains

2 cloves garlic, mashed

2 teaspoons salt

2 to 3 cups sunflower oil, for frying

**Specialty Tools:**
Kitchen thermometer

**NOTE:** Instead of the first round of frying, you can also boil the plantains. In a medium pot over medium heat, add 5 cups of water and bring to a boil. Add the plantain pieces and cook until they are soft, about 10 minutes. Dry over paper towels before mashing and frying.

1. Peel the green plantains, cut off the ends, and cut the plantains into 1½-inch pieces.

2. In a shallow bowl, add 1 cup water, the garlic, and 1 teaspoon of the salt, and set aside for 10 minutes for the flavors to mix.

3. Line a plate with paper towels. In a large pot over medium heat, place the oil and heat to 325°F. Add the plantain pieces and deep-fry for 7 minutes. They should not brown. Remove to the prepared plate to drain (see note).

4. Place a piece of parchment paper or plastic wrap on a workspace. Add each piece of cooked plantain to the paper, cover with more paper, and mash with a heavy pot until they are ¼-inch thin. Set aside until ready to fry.

5. In the same frying pot with the hot oil, over medium-high heat, increase the temperature to 375°F. Line another plate with paper towels.

6. Dip each flattened plantain into the prepared garlic water, shake off excess water, and fry for 2 to 3 minutes per side, or until crispy and lightly golden. Place onto the prepared plate and add more salt if desired before serving.

7. Serve hot with two or more of these sauces: The Magic Is Strong! Spicy Ají (page 26), Cilantro Pachanguero Salsa (page 28), Spice Lovers Peanut Ají (page 18), Uno, Dos, Tres Avocado Spread (page 31), or Gift Ceremony Tomato Salsa (page 29).

**Difficulty:** Easy
**Prep time:** 25 minutes | **Cook time:** 15 minutes
**Yield:** 4 to 6 servings (12 tajadas)
**GF, DF, V**

# Sweet Plantain Wedges
## *Tajadas de plátano maduro*

Let's turn up the volume and get ready to groove to a popular *vallenato* song!

To make *Tajadas de plátano maduro*, slice ripe plantains into wedges and fry until golden and tender. A popular dish in Colombia and other Latin American-influenced countries, it can be served as a sweet dessert or a savory side to beans, beef, or soups. Go ahead, you may have seconds to dance some more!

2 very ripe plantains (see note)

2 to 3 cups sunflower oil, for frying, plus more for brushing (if using an air fryer)

3 ounces grated white farmer cheese (about ⅓ cup)

**Specialty Tools:**

Kitchen thermometer

**NOTE:** To make this dish, it's essential to use very ripe plantains with almost black peels that are still firm to the touch. Avoid overripe plantains that feel mushy inside, as they will taste rancid. If you have green plantains, they may take up to a week to ripen naturally. Do not refrigerate them as it will affect the ripening process. It's best to buy fully ripe plantains or those that are only a couple of days away from ripening to ensure they will ripen fully without getting mushy.

1. Cut off the ends of the plantains and peel them. Cut the plantains on a diagonal into ¼-inch-thick slices.

2. To fry: Line a plate with paper towels. In a medium heavy pot over medium-high heat, bring the oil to about 350°F. Add the thin plantain slices to the oil and fry until crispy and lightly golden, 2 to 3 minutes on both sides. Remove from the oil, place on the prepared plate to drain, and serve.

3. To air fry: Brush each plantain with sunflower oil on both sides, place in the air fryer with space so they do not touch one another, and cook at 400°F for 6 minutes. Turn and cook 3 to 4 minutes more or until golden brown.

4. Sprinkle grated cheese over the wedges and serve. This is usually served as a side to many Colombian dishes, on oval wooden platters.

**Difficulty:** Easy
**Prep time:** 2 minutes | **Cook time:** 45 minutes
**Yield:** 4 to 6 servings
**GF, DF, V**

# Baked Sweet Plantain Boats
## *Plátano asado*

Say cheese, guava, or *¡La Familia Madrigal!* These Baked Sweet Plantain Boats are the vessel to a picture-perfect meal.

*Plátano asado,* a popular dish at bake-outs and barbeques, pairs well with both sweet and savory dishes. Watch as they burst into fascinating red and golden colors, gleaming like the fireworks over the amazing town in *Encanto.*

2 very ripe plantains (see note)

2 teaspoons butter, softened (for peeled baked plantains)

2 teaspoons sugar (for peeled baked plantains and plantains with cheese)

¼ pound white farmer cheese (for plantains with cheese and plantains with cheese and guava)

¼ pound guava paste (for plantains with cheese and guava)

**NOTE:** To make this dish, it's important to use very ripe plantains with almost black peels that are still firm to the touch. Avoid overripe plantains that feel mushy inside, as they will taste rancid. If you have green plantains, it may take up to a week for them to ripen naturally. Do not refrigerate them as it will affect the ripening process. It's best to buy fully ripe plantains or those that are only a couple of days away from ripening to ensure they will ripen fully without getting mushy.

1. To make in the oven or at a barbeque and bakeout: Preheat the oven or barbeque to 350°F. Place the whole, unpeeled plantains over aluminum foil. Cook on the barbeque or in the oven for 30 to 45 minutes or until they have popped out of their skin on the top and the center and the plantain has turned golden red. Remove the plantain from its skin and serve, or serve with the skin, and let each person cut their own piece.

2. To make peeled baked plantains: Preheat the oven to 350°F. Peel the plantains, place on a buttered baking pan, sprinkle with the sugar, and bake uncovered for 20 to 25 minutes or until the sugar has melted and they turn golden red-brown. Serve.

3. To make plantains with cheese: Preheat the oven to 350°F. Peel the plantains, slice into the middle lengthwise but not all the way through, and place on a buttered baking pan. Add the cheese into the slit and sprinkle with the sugar. Bake for 20 to 25 minutes or until the sugar has melted and they turn golden red-brown and serve.

4. To make plantains with cheese and guava: Preheat the oven to 350°F. Peel the plantains and slice into the middle lengthwise but not all the way through, and place on a buttered baking pan. Bake the plantains for 15 to 20 minutes. Add the cheese and pieces of guava paste in the plantain slits. Bake uncovered for 10 minutes more or until they look lightly golden-red brown.

5. All of these sweet style plantains are almost a daily staple in many Colombian homes. Serve as a side with Fiesta en el Valle Chicken Soup (page 60), Paisa Family Platter (page 73), Magic Doorknob Meat Powder (page 74), Pig in a Bag (page 86), and Home Sweet Home Rice Pudding (page 136).

Chapter

**8**

# Sweets

**Difficulty:** Easy
**Prep time:** 25 minutes | **Cook time:** 1 hour
**Yield:** 36 meringues
**GF, DF**

# Colored Mountain Meringues
## *Merenguitos*

As guests begin arriving for Antonio's gift ceremony, Luisa effortlessly carries two little girls and a coffee-drinking child on her back while holding a tray with a mountain of colorful sweets called *merenguitos*.

These petite treats are created by piping a light and sweet mixture into meringues. They are slowly baked until dry and sometimes left in warm ovens overnight to become crisp and delicious, melting in your mouth. When they're done, the best advice we can give you is to grab one before they are all gone!

1¼ cups powdered sugar

½ teaspoon powder or liquid food coloring

1 cup egg whites

⅛ teaspoon salt

⅔ plus ⅛ cup granulated sugar

**Specialty Tools:**
Pastry bags

1. Preheat the oven to 275°F.

2. In a medium bowl, mix the powdered sugar and powder food coloring (if using dry colors) and set aside. Line 3 baking sheets with parchment paper.

3. In a clean (no oil residue) and dry bowl of a mixer, beat the egg whites with 1 tablespoon water and the salt. When foamy, add the granulated sugar little by little, mixing in between each addition, for about 2 minutes. Beat until shiny and pliable (not dry) and holds stiff peaks, for about 5 to 7 minutes.

4. If your food coloring is liquid, add it to the egg mixture, but do not mix yet. Carefully pour the powdered sugar over the whites. Gently fold the mixture by hand, using a spatula, in a soft, immersive motion. Begin at the top, move to the bottom, and then back up again until all the sugar is absorbed without losing the volume of the egg whites.

5. Transfer to pastry bags and form 1-inch mound-like meringues on the prepared baking sheets. Place in the oven, reduce the temperature to 225°F, and cook for 45 minutes to 1 hour or until they develop a crust and feel dry when gently lifted from the bottom. If they are not yet ready, continue baking for 5 minutes more.

**Difficulty:** Easy

**Prep time:** 2 plus hours | **Cook time:** 15 minutes

**Yield:** 6 servings

**GF, V**

# Home Sweet Home Rice Pudding
## *Arroz con leche*

It's not hard to imagine that the Madrigal children would eagerly grab a delicious, homemade snack when they're feeling the pangs of hunger! Especially if the sweet aroma of sugar, cream, and spices wafts up the stairs of Casita. Dolores would hear a boiling sound and invite Camilo to join her in the kitchen for a cup of *arroz con leche*.

And now it's time for you to enjoy this delightful rice pudding recipe that has been passed down through generations like a treasured heirloom. Grab your spoon and get ready to indulge in the irresistible sweetness of arroz con leche!

1 cup white rice, washed

2 cinnamon sticks

1½ teaspoons salt

4 whole cloves

1½ cups whole milk

½ cup sweetened condensed milk

½ cup heavy cream

⅓ cup sugar

¼ cup raisins

Powdered cinnamon, for serving

1. In a large medium heavy pot, add 4 cups water, the rice, cinnamon sticks, ¾ teaspoon of the salt, and the cloves, and mix, cover, and set aside for 1 hour.

2. Keeping the pot covered, place over medium-high heat, and bring to a simmer. Uncover, decrease the temperature to medium-low, and simmer for 1 hour and 10 minutes.

3. In a small pot over medium heat, add the milk, condensed milk, cream, sugar, remaining ¾ teaspoon salt, and the raisins, and cook, stirring, for 10 minutes. Turn off the heat, pour this milk mixture into the pot with rice, and stir.

4. Transfer to a 9-by-13-inch baking dish for 15 minutes to begin to cool. Cover with parchment paper touching the pudding to avoid a crust from forming and refrigerate. Serve cold in tall glasses, ice-cream cups, or wine glasses, with some cinnamon sprinkled on top.

**Difficulty:** Easy
**Prep time:** 5 minutes | **Cook time:** 0 minutes
**Yield:** 8 servings
**GF, V**

# Guava and Cheese Mini Bites
## *Bocadillo con queso*

These sweet mini bites are called *casado* or *matrimonio*, meaning wed or wedding. A chunk of guava paste and a thick slice of white cheese are married to create this quick Colombian dessert called *Bocadillo con queso*.

They're widely known in all regions of Colombia and would surely be a favorite of Mariano Guzmán, who has so much love inside—especially for these!

1 pound white farmer cheese

1 pound guava paste, or guava squares

**Specialty Tools:**

Decorative toothpicks

1. Slice the cheese and guava paste into ½-by-½-inch squares. Pin one on top of the other with decorative toothpicks and serve.

**Difficulty:** Easy
**Prep time:** 25 minutes | **Cook time:** 1½ hours
**Yield:** 6 to 8 servings
**GF, DF, V, V+**

# Guava Treasure Cups
## *Cascos de guayaba*

What a wonderful discovery it was when Antonio opened the door of his magical room in Encanto and uncovered a huge tropical forest inside of Casita.

If you like surprises, prepare to be amazed by this tropical fruit that is green on the outside and pink on the inside! To make these Guava Treasure Cups, we first halve and remove the seeds from the fruits. Then, we cook them in sweet syrup with a touch of tangy lemon. This brings out their natural pinkish-red hue and gives them a scrumptious taste.

Fill them with ice cream, cheese, or your favorite treat for a tasty treasure worth discovering.

2 pounds fresh guavas (about 8 guavas)

1 lemon

3 cups sugar

1. Peel the guavas, cut them in half, and remove the seeds. This will result in two tiny bowl-shaped pieces from each guava.

2. Cut the peel from the lemon with a vegetable peeler into ½-inch-wide strips.

3. In a medium pot over medium-high heat, add the sugar, lemon peel, and 3 cups water, simmer, and mix to dissolve the sugar. Add the guavas, turn the heat down to medium-low, cover, and cook for 20 minutes. Uncover and continue cooking for 1 hour or until the guavas look bright colored and almost glisten. Set aside to cool, transfer to a container, and refrigerate. Serve cold.

4. These delectable guava cups can be served with sweet or savory sides, such as creamy white farmer cheese or filled with a scoop of refreshing ice cream.

**Difficulty:** Medium
**Prep time:** 25 minutes | **Cook time:** 25 minutes
**Yield:** 12 servings, 24 bites
**GF, DF, V, V+**

# Coconut Fudgies
## *Cocadas blancas*

These tasty Coconut Fudgies, often sold during carnival, on street carts, and on beach walks, are the true taste of a tropical paradise.

They're cooked to a perfectly crispy exterior and a chewy, coconut-filled center. Our recipe offers bite-size one-inch servings—perfect for kids and grown-ups!

1 cup coconut water (see note)

¾ cup sugar

2 cups freshly grated coconut (grated on the largest hole) (see note)

**NOTE:** The coconut and water can come from one large coconut.

1. Line a baking sheet with parchment paper. In a heavy, large, shallow pot over medium heat, place the coconut water and sugar and cook for 10 minutes or until you have a light-colored, almost caramel syrup.

2. Decrease the temperature to low to prevent the sugar from turning into golden caramel, add the grated coconut, and immediately start mixing with a wooden spoon. Keep mixing until you can see the bottom of the pot, about 15 minutes.

3. On the prepared baking sheet, drop 1-inch spoonfuls of the mixture to create mounds. Allow them to cool completely until dry at the bottom, then peel off each mound from the parchment paper, and serve.

# Wobbly Andean Coffee Crème
## Flan de café

Take the grown-ups on a sensory journey to the Andean mountains with this coffee custard dessert topped with a coffee caramel sauce.

Like Bruno's improvised hideaway is conveniently located next to Casita's kitchen, Colombia's diverse geography offers ideal conditions for cultivating coffee in small family farms called fincas. Surrounded by mountains, the families in the magical town in *Encanto* would surely delight in the unforgettable taste of our *Flan de café*.

1½ cups sugar

1½ tablespoons freeze-dried coffee

8 eggs

1 cup sweetened condensed milk

1 cup heavy whipping cream, very cold

1 tablespoon vanilla extract

**Specialty Tools:**
9-inch round glass baking dish or cake pan

1. Preheat the oven to 300°F.

2. Place 1 cup of the sugar and 1 cup water in a small heavy pot over high heat. Once it starts to boil, stir to dissolve the sugar. Decrease the heat to medium and cook for 10 minutes or until light golden in color. Pour immediately into the baking dish or cake pan. Swirl to cover the bottom and sides of the baking dish. Be careful, as the caramel is very hot. Set aside.

3. Place the remaining ½ cup sugar, coffee, eggs, condensed milk, cream, and vanilla in a blender and mix for 1 to 2 minutes. Gently pour the flan mixture into the baking dish.

4. Place the baking dish into a larger baking dish and add water to the larger baking dish to a depth of 1 inch to create a bain-marie. Bake for 1 hour.

5. Remove from the oven and from the outer pan containing the water. Pass the pointed end of a knife around the sides of the flan to help release it. Set aside for at least 10 minutes or until you can comfortably touch the baking dish with your hands and not get burned. Place your serving dish upside down over the baking dish and quickly flip the whole thing over. Remove the baking dish.

6. Serve at room temperature or chill and serve cold.

**Difficulty:** Easy
**Prep time:** 8 minutes | **Cook time:** 15 minutes
**Yield:** ¾ cup
**GF, V**

# Glowing Caramel with Fresh Cheese
## *Melado con cuajada*

Don Osvaldo's "not special special" basket for Mirabel included four dazzling blocks of raw sugar called *panela*. Handmade from the sweet juice of sugar cane, these golden treasures are capable of shape-shifting to a radiant red caramel known as *melado*, or *melao* for short.

When fresh farmer cheese is generously topped with *melado*, this Colombian dessert transforms into a sweet gift that would impress Mirabel herself.

½ pound solid panela (see page 13)

1 cinnamon stick

1 lime, peel and juice

1 pound fresh-milk cheese

Mint leaves or lemon tree leaves, for garnish

1. In a small pot over medium heat, place 1½ cups water, the panela, cinnamon stick, and lime peel and cook until all the panela has dissolved.

2. Increase the heat to medium-high and bring to a boil. As soon as it boils (about 2 minutes), decrease the heat to medium and simmer for about 5 minutes until it starts to thicken, and lightly coats the back of a wooden spoon. Add the lime juice, stir, and set aside to cool.

3. Slice the fresh-milk cheese into 2-ounce triangles and pour 2 tablespoons of the syrup over the cheese. Serve as individual portions on small dessert plates, about 1 ounce of cheese in a triangular form and with plenty of sauce on top. Garnish with a mint or lemon tree leaf.

**Difficulty:** Medium
**Prep time:** 25 minutes | **Cook time:** 15 minutes
**Yield:** 12 servings
**GF, V**

# The Real Gift Custard Delight
## *Natilla*

This cherished gift from Colombia's Antioquia region is typically enjoyed during the holidays when presents await under the tree to spark joy and traditional Christmas songs called villancicos fill the air.

Kids unwrapping presents feel the same mystery and excitement as when the Madrigal children and grandchildren touched each doorknob to discover their magical gift.

The Real Gift Custard Delight is a semi-sweet dessert made with milk, panela, and cinnamon sticks cooked over low heat. It's time for you to discover why Natilla is the real gift.

2½ tablespoons butter, plus more for greasing

3½ cups whole milk

½ pound panela, grated or firmly pressed dark brown sugar (see page 13)

2 cinnamon sticks

¼ teaspoon baking soda

⅛ teaspoon salt

¾ cup plus 2 tablespoons cornstarch

Sugar confetti stars, for garnish (optional)

Ground cinnamon, for garnish

1 orange, peeled and cut into pieces, for garnish

### Specialty Tools:

8-by-8-inch square 2-inch deep baking dish

1. Grease a square baking dish with butter.

2. In a small, heavy pot over very low heat, place 2 cups of the milk, the panela, cinnamon sticks, baking soda, and salt. Mix until the panela has completely dissolved, but do not boil.

3. In a medium bowl, mix the remaining milk and the cornstarch, add to the pot, increase the heat to medium-high, and mix continuously with a flat spatula or wooden spoon until the mix thickens and you can see the bottom of the pan, about 15 minutes.

4. Remove immediately from the heat, add the butter, stir, remove the cinnamon sticks, and pour into the prepared baking dish. Allow to cool completely, cut into squares, scoop out the squares, and serve at room temperature.

5. To serve, sprinkle with confetti stars, if using, ground cinnamon, and the orange peel.

# Extra Special Candy Swirls
## *Alfeñiques*

*Alfeñiques* are featured in the "not special special" basket Don Osvaldo gives to Mirabel at the beginning of the movie. These delightful treats that look like tall lollipops are made with a powdered sugar mixture shaped around wooden sticks and then covered with coconut flakes, quinoa puffs, and walnuts.

In Colombia, particularly in the city of Cali, kids get these amazing baskets called *macetas* that are filled with candy, paper crafts, and cute little toys. It's such a fun way to surprise and celebrate with the little ones!

2 egg whites

⅛ teaspoon salt

1 pound plus ½ cup powdered sugar

2 teaspoons cinnamon

1 teaspoon vanilla

1 tablespoon lime juice

2 cups of quinoa puffs

¾ cup ground roasted walnuts

¾ cup dry coconut flakes

**Specialty Tools:**

1 large silicone pastry bag (optional)

Bamboo or wooden skewers

1. Line a baking sheet with parchment paper or a silicone baking mat. Place the egg whites and salt in the bowl of a stand mixer, or a medium mixing bowl if using a handheld mixer, and mix at medium-low speed until frothy, about 2 minutes. Reduce the speed to low, add the powdered sugar, and mix at medium speed for 5 minutes. Stop the mixer, add the cinnamon, vanilla, and lime juice, and mix until well distributed, about 1 minute. Stop the mixer, and place a dough hook, if available. Otherwise, mix by hand. Add 1¼ cups of the quinoa puffs, ⅓ cup of the ground roasted walnuts, and ⅓ cup of the dry coconut flakes, and mix on low speed for about 1 minute until everything is well combined.

2. Transfer the mix to a large silicone pastry bag or onto parchment paper on a workplace. Place the remaining quinoa puffs, walnuts, and coconut flakes on separate 6-inch shallow plates.

3.  To make the candy with a pastry bag: Place the mixture into a large silicone pastry bag and cut a ¾-inch opening. Pipe the mixture into 3-inch-long logs on the prepared baking sheets. You will need strong hands as it is somewhat thick. Roll or sprinkle quinoa, walnuts, and coconut flakes over the tops and sides of each log. Insert bamboo or wooden skewers into the center of each candy roll. Use your hands to reshape them into various forms if desired. Set them aside overnight on parchment paper to allow them to dry and set.

4.  To make the candy on parchment paper: Divide the batter into 3 parts, keeping them covered with a kitchen towel. Roll each portion of batter into two 2-inch-wide-by-8-inch-long rolls. Cut each roll into a total of 36 pieces and shape them into logs, triangles, or rounds. Sprinkle or roll the remaining quinoa, ground walnuts, and coconut flakes onto the candies, ensuring all sides are covered. Insert bamboo or wooden skewers into the center of each candy and set them aside overnight to dry.

# Mystical Gift Cookies
## *Polvorosas*

Experience a delectable vision of joy that will melt in your mouth! *Polvorosas* are so delicious because they have a crunchy and powdery texture, which is achieved by gently combining clarified butter.

Make a big batch of these cookies, as they are sure to disappear quickly, just like sand through the hourglass on Bruno's door.

½ pound clarified butter, in chunks

¼ cup granulated sugar

½ cup powdered sugar, plus extra for garnishing

1 teaspoon pure vanilla extract

2¼ cups all-purpose flour

**NOTE:** When they reach room temperature, you can store these cookies in tightly sealed containers or jars for up to 1 week.

1. Preheat the oven to 300°F. Cover 3 baking sheets with silicone baking mats or parchment paper.

2. In the bowl of a stand mixer, or a large mixing bowl if using a hand mixer, beat the butter and granulated sugar on medium speed for 5 minutes. Add the powdered sugar and mix for 5 minutes more. Add the vanilla and mix for 30 seconds. Stop the machine, add the flour, and decrease the speed to low. Mix for 1 minute only.

3. Scoop out 1 tablespoon portions of dough, roll into balls, and place them onto the prepared baking sheets, spaced 2 inches apart from each other. Flatten to form dome shapes and bake for 15 to 20 minutes or until they feel dry in the center. They will be just lightly golden all over. Dust with powdered sugar and serve.

**Difficulty:** Medium
**Prep time:** 10 minutes | **Cook time:** 35 minutes
**Yield:** 8 servings
**GF, V**

# Coconut Fudgies for Pepa's Happiest Mood
## *Panelitas*

*Panelitas* are treats that resemble fudge cookies and are a warm and bright combination of raw sugar (*panela*), milk, vanilla extract, and sometimes coconut! Little mounds of sweetness and crunch are left to solidify at room temperature. If flattened, they become coconut fudge coins!

Our recipe is simply scrumptious and has the power to brighten up even Pepa's gloomiest day. So go ahead and indulge—there's no need to be shy about licking your fingers clean!

2 cups whole milk

½ cup white rice

1 lime peel

⅛ teaspoon salt

1½ cups grated or granulated panela or raw brown sugar

2½ cups finely grated fresh coconut (from 1 coconut)

1 teaspoon vanilla extract

1. Line a baking sheet with parchment paper or a silicone baking mat.

2. In a small pot over medium heat, add 1 cup of the milk, the rice, lime peel, and salt. Bring to a boil, reduce the temperature to low, cover, and cook for 20 minutes. Remove the lime peel, mash the mixture with a potato masher or ricer, or quickly process for 10 seconds, and return to the pot.

3. Increase the heat to medium, add the remaining 1 cup milk, the panela, grated coconut, and vanilla extract, and cook until it thickens and you can see the bottom of the pot, about 10 minutes.

4. Remove from the heat and scoop out tablespoons of the fudge onto the prepared baking sheet. Allow to cool.

5. Place in airtight containers when cool and serve at room temperature.

# Chapter
## 9

# Drinks and Fruits

# Grown-Ups' Morning Boost
## *Café con leche, tinto, and pintado*

Colombian coffee has been known worldwide for its rich taste, vibrant aroma, and evergreen tropical notes since it was introduced to the region three centuries ago. Coffee beans are carefully nurtured by loving hands, mountain breezes, and fertile soil, and picked at the correct ripeness. They offer a smooth, rounded flavor that captivates the world.

In Colombian households, coffee is offered as a welcoming gesture at any time of the day. It symbolizes warmth, hospitality, and the start of meaningful conversations. For families like the Madrigals, the morning ritual begins with a *tinto* and a glass of water before breakfast is served. This elevated sense of tradition is guaranteed to suit any preference, so you can add milk to make *café con leche* or a touch of cream to enjoy a *pintao*.

In *Encanto*, a young boy is constantly seen with a cup of coffee, radiating endless energy. Despite Mirabel's reminder that children shouldn't drink coffee, he persists in running around with it, adding a touch of charm and humor to the story. This highlights the cultural significance of coffee in Colombia, even within the inspirational world of *Encanto*.

Traditionally, Colombian coffee is served in three ways: *tinto*, *pintado (or pintao)*, and *café con leche*.

# *Café con leche*

**Difficulty:** Easy
**Prep time:** 1 minute | **Cook time:** 3 minutes
**Yield:** 1 serving
**GF, V**

*Latte* or *café con leche* is a breakfast beverage made with equal parts milk and black coffee.

For great consistency, it's best to use instant freeze-dried or powdered coffee. It's commonly consumed in the morning or in the afternoons with a side of pastries or baked treats.

1 teaspoon instant coffee powder

1 teaspoon sugar

1 cup warm milk

1. In a mug or 8-ounce coffee cup, pour the instant coffee powder, sugar, and warm milk. Mix and serve.

*continued on page 156*

*continued from page 155*

**Difficulty:** Easy
**Prep time:** 1 minute | **Cook time:** 3 minutes
**Yield:** 4 servings
**GF, DF, V, V+**

# Tinto

Black coffee, or tinto, was traditionally made by pouring boiled water over a handmade fabric filter filled with ground coffee into a serving pot. Nowadays, it is mostly made using a drip coffee maker.

Tinto is often served in 2-to-3-ounce cups with a glass of water on the side, and it's a significant part of the daily routine in homes and offices, where drinking black coffee helps to clear the mind, or perhaps when Pepa and her sister Julieta sit in rocking chairs in Casita's foyer as they sip tinto on cloudless afternoons.

2 cups water

2 tablespoons ground coffee

**Specialty Tools:**

1 cloth coffee filter

1. In a small pot over medium-high heat, bring the water to a boil. Set aside for 2 minutes. Place the coffee filter over a jar and add the ground coffee.
2. Place the filter with the coffee into the hot water and leave it there for 1 minute. Remove the filter with the ground coffee and serve the prepared black coffee in 2-to-3-ounce cups called tinto cups.

# Pintado

**Difficulty:** Easy
**Prep time:** 1 minute | **Cook time:** 3 minutes
**Yield:** 1 serving
**GF, V**

Pintado is typically prepared at the table, allowing each person to choose how much milk to add, usually 1 to 2 teaspoons. It is served as a post-meal beverage and might be a great energy boost for Luisa when she needs to resume chores after a big lunch.

2 to 3 ounces prepared black coffee

½ tablespoon warm milk

1. In an espresso-size cup, pour the coffee, add the warm milk, and serve.

**Difficulty:** Medium
**Prep time:** 10 minutes | **Cook time:** 10 minutes
**Yield:** 4 servings
**GF, V**

# Heartwarming Cocoa Hug
## *Chocolate caliente*

On chilly mornings, Colombians dissolve sweetened chocolate squares into milk heated in a traditional pot called a chocolatera, mixed using a wooden whisk called a molinillo. Nowadays, a blender is also used to prepare this delicious beverage. Hot chocolate is a delightful drink that can be enjoyed at any time of the day.

The chilly evening wind blowing from the mountains surrounding the town in Encanto would invite a cozy Madrigal sisters' get-together over a cup of Chocolate caliente. This heartwarming moment might be strong enough to save the family miracle!

This chocolatey beverage, suitable for all ages, is often served at breakfast. It pairs harmoniously with Enchanting Scrambled Eggs (page 25), Behind the Walls Corn Arepas (page 37), Cheesy Arepas (page 38), Sweet Corncakes (page 40), Baked Cassava Bread (page 51), or fresh white farmer cheese.

4 ounces sweetened table chocolate

4 cups milk, or 2 cups water and 2 cups milk

2 tablespoons sugar

1. Chop the chocolate into small pieces.

2. In a small pot add the milk, chopped chocolate, and sugar. Place pot over medium heat and mix until the milk begins to smoke but does not boil. Transfer to a blender and mix to create a frothy consistency. Serve hot.

**Difficulty:** Medium
**Prep time:** 10 minutes | **Cook time:** 0 minutes
**Yield:** 2 servings
**GF, DF*, V, V+***

# Passion Fruit Butterfly Bliss
## *Jugo y sorbete de maracuyá*

A yellow butterfly appeared in Bruno's vision, leading the way to a bright future for Mirabel and Alma's family, whom they love and protect passionately.

The bliss and profound joy of that moment must be celebrated! We present you with a fruit as mystic and full of passion as the Amazon Rainforest itself. Passion fruit, also known as *maracuyá* or *parcha* in some Latin American countries, is a versatile tropical fruit that can be used for a variety of dishes, including cold juice, sweet sorbets, smoothies, sauces, jellies, and desserts like mousse and cheesecake.

¼ cup passion fruit pulp
(1 large passion fruit)

2 tablespoons sugar

3 cups water or 2 cups milk and
1 cup water

1 cup crushed ice

1. In a blender, place the passion fruit pulp. Blend for 3 seconds, pass through a sieve, and place the remaining liquid back into the blender. Discard the seeds. Add the sugar, water or milk, and ice, and blend to a smoothie. Pour into two glasses and serve.

**NOTES:** This same recipe works for the *curuba* fruit.

This recipe is dairy-free and vegan if the milk is omitted.

**Difficulty:** Medium
**Prep time:** 10 minutes | **Cook time:** 0 minutes
**Yield:** 2 servings of each fruit
GF, DF*, V, V+*

# Shape-Shifting Fruit Treats
## Jugos, Sorbetes y Paletas

As there are no limits to Camilo and his ability to shape-shift into anyone he chooses in *Encanto*, there are also many ways to combine fruits to transform them into delicious, healthy, and natural treats.

In Colombia, a variety of colorful and sweet native fruits burst with flavor. Tropical fruits like mango, guava, pineapple, or soursop are great options for these recipes, and when mixed with lime, the fruit undergoes a touch of mouthwatering magic.

Whether you choose Colombian or local fruits that are available to you, you can be confident they will beautifully complement the zesty lime juice, adding a sprinkle of enchantment to this delightful concoction. It's the magic of *Encanto* transformed to please the crowds!

2 cups peeled, seeded, diced papaya
(about ⅓ papaya or 1 Hawaiian papaya)

2 teaspoons lime juice

1 cup water, or ½ cup water and
½ cup milk

1 tablespoon sugar (optional)

1 cup ice

1. In a blender, place the papaya, lime juice, and water, and blend. Add sugar if deemed necessary, as it will depend on the sweetness of the fruit. Add the ice, pulse the blender, and serve as juice or freeze as Popsicles, or paletas.

**NOTES:** When milk is used in the preparation, whether it's vegan or dairy, these are referred to as *sorbetes*, a term that signifies smoothies made with milk.

This recipe is dairy-free and vegan if the milk is omitted.

# Drinkable Yogurt Vision
## *Kumis*

Long ago, in enchanting lands surrounding green mountains like the magical town in *Encanto*, this kefir-style milk drink was homemade and served cold for breakfast or an afternoon snack. *Kumis* is sold today in stores and enjoyed as a healthy drink by most kids and grown-ups in Colombia.

This drinkable yogurt is created by fermenting whole milk with lime. The green power of this citrus fruit evokes a delightful and magical vision of tasty glee. But remember, you can't hurry the future! Note that this recipe takes two days to prepare.

2 quarts whole milk

3 tablespoons lime juice

2 cups sugar

1 teaspoon cinnamon

**NOTE:** In very hot climates where kitchens are above 78°F, the milk can be refrigerated after 6 to 8 hours, rather than being set aside overnight (about 12 hours).

### Day 1

1. In a large glass or stainless-steel bowl, add the milk and lime juice, cover with a damp kitchen towel, and set aside overnight (see note).

### Day 2

2. In a blender, blend the milk mixture with the sugar and cinnamon for 1 to 2 minutes or until it reaches the consistency of smooth yogurt. Refrigerate for 24 hours before serving. It is best after 3 days and can be kept for up to 7 days.

**Difficulty:** Medium
**Prep time:** 35 minutes | **Cook time:** 30 minutes (for syrups)
**Yield:** 8 servings, and one cup of each syrup
**GF, V**

# Town Kids Shaved Ice
## *Cholado or Raspado*

Food carts and street vendors are found everywhere in Colombia's small villages and large cities alike. One of the classic and favorite treats you might find at these carts is known as *cholado* in the southern Pacific or *raspado* in the northern Caribbean regions.

A huge block of ice changes its shape as quickly as Camilo Madrigal would, piling up like snow on a plastic or paper cup to then flavored with colored syrup, freshly cut fruit, and condensed milk, magically transforming the shaved ice into a delicious treat.

Picking from the array of rainbow-like flavors and toppings is as difficult as choosing your favorite color in Isabela's new dress design when she discovered her true self.

### For the tamarind syrup:

1 pound tamarind pulp with seeds (available at most Asian or Latin grocery stores)

1 cup sugar

1 cinnamon stick (optional)

### For the passion fruit syrup:

1 cup fresh passion fruit pulp (from about 4 passion fruits), or frozen, unsweetened, thawed pulp

1 cup granulated sugar

1 tablespoon lime juice

### For the strawberry soda syrup:

12 ounces strawberry soda

### For two servings:

1½ cups shaved ice

¼ cup unsweetened fruit pulp (optional)

2 tablespoons Tamarind, Passion Fruit, or Strawberry Soda Syrup

2 tablespoons sweet condensed milk

### To make the tamarind syrup:

1. In a small pot, place the tamarind pulp and 2 cups water or enough to cover the pulp. Set aside overnight or break it into pieces and cook as follows. Place the pot with the pulp and water over medium heat and simmer for 30 minutes, or until the water thickens and turns golden brown. Allow it to cool for 10 minutes, then pass it through a sieve while mixing with a wooden spoon to separate the pulp from the seeds. Set the seeds aside. Transfer the warm pulp back to the pot.

2. Add ½ cup of the sugar to the pulp in the pot. Stir the mixture over low heat for about 2 minutes to dissolve the sugar. Taste the mixture to assess its sweetness. The pulp's sourness can vary. Add the remaining ½ cup sugar, if you deem it necessary. This is the syrup.

### To make the passion fruit syrup:

3. In a small bowl, add the passion fruit pulp and 1 cup water, stir well, and strain through a sieve to remove any seeds. Blend it with the water and strain the pulp through a sieve to remove any seeds, while retaining the mixture.

4. In a small saucepan over medium-high heat, add the passion fruit mixture and sugar, and simmer for 15 minutes until a thin syrup forms. Remove from the heat, add the lime juice, and allow it to cool.

### To make the strawberry syrup:

5. In a small pot, over medium-high heat, place the strawberry soda. Bring to a boil and simmer until halved in volume.

### To assemble two servings:

6. Place ¼ of the shaved ice into each one of the two cups. Drizzle each with some syrup and add a spoonful of fruit pulp, if using. Then add half the remaining shaved ice to each cup, and shape into a round form using a rounded cup. Finally, drizzle the mound with additional syrup, condensed milk, and a spoonful of fruit to each cup (if using it).

**Difficulty:** Medium
**Prep time:** 25 minutes | **Cook time:** 20 minutes
**Yield:** 8 to 10 servings
**GF, DF\*, V, V+\***

# Fruity Fiesta Medley
## Tutti frutti or Salpicón

Each corner of the town in Encanto is a colorful display of vibrant details inspired by our beautiful country's diversity.

Apart from being this recipe's name, the word *salpicón* could be used in Colombia to point out something that includes a wide variety of different elements, food, and even people! And when you combine the assorted flavors and textures of tropical fruits, diced small, and packed in their own juicy sweetness, you'd certainly feel as if you tasted a rainbow!

Our Fruity Fiesta Medley is best enjoyed chilled in individual cups for a naturally refreshing party at home. It would surely become a favorite among the Madrigal kids, especially if it's topped with a scoop of vanilla ice cream.

3 cups finely diced papaya (about 1 medium, or 3 Hawaiian papayas)

3 cups finely diced watermelon (about ½ watermelon)

1 teaspoon sugar (optional)

1 teaspoon lemon juice (optional)

2 cups finely diced pineapple (about ½ pineapple)

2 cups finely diced mango

2 bananas, chopped

8 to 10 small scoops vanilla ice cream (optional)

1. In a blender, blend 2 cups of the papaya or watermelon and ½ cup water into a juice consistency. Taste to assess sweetness and add the optional sugar if you think it is needed. When using papaya for the juice, add the lemon juice to make it tastier.

2. In a large bowl, place the remaining papaya and/or watermelon, the pineapple, and mango. Pour the papaya juice over the fruit, add the banana, and mix. Serve cold with or without ice cream. Keep refrigerated.

**NOTES:** Two cups fresh orange juice can be used instead of papaya juice.

This recipe is dairy-free and vegan if served without ice cream, or by using your favorite dairy-free substitute.

**Difficulty:** Medium
**Prep time:** 15 minutes | **Cook time:** 0 minutes
**Yield:** One 12-ounce juice
**GF, DF, V, V+**

# Lulo Juice

*Lulo*, a green kiwi-like fruit with an orange exterior, is tart and acidic, which makes it a fantastic juice. If you purchase *lulo* pulp, it might be sweetened so tasting is recommended.

¼ cup peeled lulo (about 1 to 2 lulos)

2 tablespoons sugar

1 cup crushed ice

1. In a blender mix the lulo and sugar until the sugar has dissolved. Add 1 cup water and the ice and blend. Pour into a glass and serve.

# Sweet and Tart Beverage
## *Lulada*

**Difficulty:** Medium
**Prep time:** 15 minutes | **Cook time:** 0 minutes
**Yield:** 9 servings (one large pitcher)
**GF, DF, V, V+**

Growing up in Casita together, Julieta, Bruno, and Pepa certainly had plenty of fun. Bruno would predict the future for entertainment, Pepa would learn how to handle her weather-changing emotions, and Julieta would experiment in the kitchen with ingredients that would make her healing recipes taste delicious.

One of these tasty creations could be *lulada*, made with *lulo*, a tart, and refreshing tropical fruit. When perfectly ripe, no peeling is needed for the *lulo*. Simply cut it in half and gently push the skin to reveal a mesmerizing sight as it drops into your glass. After adding ice and quickly stirring with a long spoon, enjoy a rollercoaster of sweet and tart flavors that could wake Alma Madrigal from her afternoon nap to join her grandchildren in their magical games.

3 cups fresh and peeled lulos (about 8 to 10 lulos)

6 tablespoons sugar

2½ cups crushed ice

1. In a medium bowl, place the lulos and mash them. Add the sugar and set aside 5 minutes until they absorb the sugar.

2. Fill tall glasses with crushed ice and divide the lulo mixture among them. Serve immediately.

**Difficulty:** Easy
**Prep time:** 15 to 20 minutes
**Cook time:** 0 minutes
**Yield:** 1 large platter | **GF, DF, V, V+**

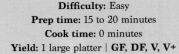

# Bountiful Harvest Platter
## *Bandeja de frutas*

Inspired by *Encanto*'s stunning food buffets and tables, this edible grand centerpiece captures the spirit of sharing and celebration reminiscent of many Colombian and Latin families that, just like *la familia* Madrigal, enjoy gathering to commemorate unity and traditions.

Our Bountiful Harvest Platter embodies a sustainable approach, ensuring that every element is entirely edible and contributes to the table's natural beauty. Every ready-to-eat fruit is carefully chosen based on its freshness, color, succulence, size, and shape, ensuring a delightful sensory experience for both the eyes and taste buds.

We invite you to feast on the beauty of each element representing Colombia's vibrant and rich diversity. The harmony between nature's bountiful offerings and the creative arrangement culminates in a truly remarkable and delectable experience.

1 pineapple, with its crown

1 papaya

5 bananas

5 tangerines

3 guavas

3 mangoes

3 passion fruits

1 bunch purple grapes

Leaves from a plant or palm

Dry herbs (rosemary, oregano, thyme), for amazing aroma

1. Buy your favorite fruit and separate it by size. Keep bananas and other medium-size fruit onthe side.

2. Place the larger fruit in the center, keep the leaves and pineapple crown as part of the decoration.

3. Fill the empty spaces with smaller fruit, leaving some fruit bunches like grapes or Colombian palm fruit called corozo to fall off the sides.

4. By making sure colors are varied, you create an amazing centerpiece that is later eaten by families like the Madrigals.

5. Enjoy the colorful bounty of Colombian fruit whilst it ripens at home.

# Metric Conversion Chart

## Kitchen Measurements

| CUPS | TABLESPOONS | TEASPOONS | FLUID OUNCES |
|------|-------------|-----------|--------------|
| ⅟₁₆ cup | 1 tbsp | 3 tsp | ½ fl oz |
| ⅛ cup | 2 tbsp | 6 tsp | 1 fl oz |
| ¼ cup | 4 tbsp | 12 tsp | 2 fl oz |
| ⅓ cup | 5½ tbsp | 16 tsp | 2⅔ fl oz |
| ½ cup | 8 tbsp | 24 tsp | 4 fl oz |
| ⅔ cup | 10⅔ tbsp | 32 tsp | 5⅓ fl oz |
| ¾ cup | 12 tbsp | 36 tsp | 6 fl oz |
| 1 cup | 16 tbsp | 48 tsp | 8 fl oz |

| GALLONS | QUARTS | PINTS | CUPS | FLUID OUNCES |
|---------|--------|-------|------|--------------|
| ⅟₁₆ gal | ¼ qt | ½ pt | 1 cup | 8 fl oz |
| ⅛ gal | ½ qt | 1 pt | 2 cups | 16 fl oz |
| ¼ gal | 1 qt | 2 pt | 4 cups | 32 fl oz |
| ½ gal | 2 qt | 4 pt | 8 cups | 64 fl oz |
| 1 gal | 4 qt | 8 pt | 16 cups | 128 fl oz |

## Weight

| GRAMS | OUNCES |
|-------|--------|
| 14 g | ½ oz |
| 28 g | 1 oz |
| 57 g | 2 oz |
| 85 g | 3 oz |
| 113 g | 4 oz |
| 142 g | 5 oz |
| 170 g | 6 oz |
| 283 g | 10 oz |
| 397 g | 14 oz |
| 454 g | 16 oz |
| 907 g | 32 oz |

## Oven Temperatures

| FAHRENHEIT | CELSIUS |
|------------|---------|
| 200 °F | 93 °C |
| 225 °F | 107 °C |
| 250 °F | 121 °C |
| 275 °F | 135 °C |
| 300 °F | 149 °C |
| 325 °F | 163 °C |
| 350 °F | 177 °C |
| 375 °F | 191 °C |
| 400 °F | 204 °C |
| 425 °F | 218 °C |
| 450 °F | 232 °C |

## Length

| IMPERIAL | METRIC |
|----------|--------|
| 1 in | 2.5 cm |
| 2 in | 5 cm |
| 4 in | 10 cm |
| 6 in | 15 cm |
| 8 in | 20 cm |
| 10 in | 25 cm |
| 12 in | 30 cm |

# Notes

## INSIGHT
### EDITIONS

PO Box 3088
San Rafael, CA 94912
www.insighteditions.com

Find us on Facebook: www.facebook.com/InsightEditions
Follow us on Instagram: @insighteditions

ISBN: 979-8-88663-350-4
Gift Edition: 979-8-88663-352-8

Publisher: Raoul Goff
VP, Group Publisher: Vanessa Lopez
VP, Creative: Chrissy Kwasnik
VP, Manufacturing: Alix Nicholaeff
Publishing Director: Jamie Thompson
Senior Designer: Judy Wiatrek Trum
Senior Editor: Anna Wostenberg
Editorial Assistant: Alecsander Zapata
Executive Project Editor: Maria Spano
Production Associate: Deena Hashem
Senior Production Manager, Subsidiary Rights: Lina s Palma-Temena

Photographer: Ted Thomas
Food and Prop Stylist: Elena P. Craig
Assistant Food Stylist: Patricia Parrish
Assistant Food Stylist: Wesley Anderson

  REPLANTED PAPER

Insight Editions, in association with Roots of Peace, will plant two trees for each tree used in the manufacturing of this book. Roots of Peace is an internationally renowned humanitarian organization dedicated to eradicating land mines worldwide and converting war-torn lands into productive farms and wildlife habitats. Roots of Peace will plant two million fruit and nut trees in Afghanistan and provide farmers there with the skills and support necessary for sustainable land use.

Manufactured in China by Insight Editions

10 9 8 7 6 5 4 3 2 1